ANN DESBOROUGH

The Chicken
AND THE EGG

A COMPREHENSIVE GUIDE TO THE WORLD OF CHICKENS

ANN DESBOROUGH

The Chicken and the Egg

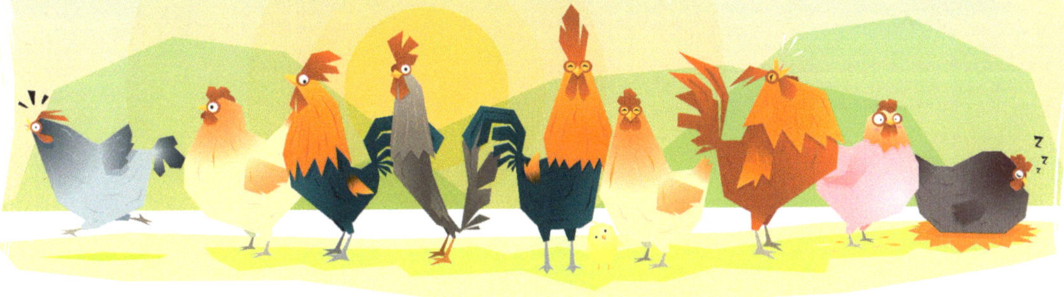

A COMPREHENSIVE GUIDE TO THE WORLD OF CHICKENS

MEREO

Published by Mereo

Mereo is an imprint of Memoirs Publishing

1A The Market Place Cirencester Gloucestershire GL7 2PR
info@memoirsbooks.co.uk | www.memoirspublishing.com

The Chicken and the Egg

All Rights Reserved. Copyright © Ann Desborough

No part of this book may be reproduced or transmitted in any form or by any means, graphic, electronic, or mechanical, including photocopying, recording, taping or by any information storage or retrieval system, without the permission in writing from the copyright holder. The right of Robina Hutchinson to be identified as the author of this work has been asserted in accordance with the Copyright, Designs and Patents Act 1988 sections 77 and 78.

Design and artwork - Ray Lipscombe

The views expressed in this work are solely those of the author and do not necessarily reflect the views of the publisher, and the publisher hereby disclaims any responsibility for them.

ISBN: 978-1-86151-845-3

Dedicated to all those children, grandchildren and great-grandchildren who shared magic moments with me at my kitchen table cracking eggs, separating yolks from whites and turning them into breakfasts, lunches, high teas and dinners. If you have some free time, a spare grandchild and half a dozen eggs....
HAPPY DAYS!

Hannah, Peter, Jacob C, Devon, Matthew, Jacob, William, Teddy

The Chicken and the Egg

Contents

CHICKENS AND ME – SORRY, CHICKENS AND I

A child in Underwood	1
Becoming eggbound	5
Chickens and gamekeepers	7
What do you know about poultry?	9
Chickens and their eggs	9
Yum-Yum Corner: Learning to cook eggs	11
Four ways to cook very fresh eggs for tea	12
Research: Finding out about shop-bought eggs	15
Fresh eggs experiment	16
Rosehip syrup	17
Chicken Little	19

LIFE IN THE YARD

Finding out about free-range hens and bantams	22
Hens in barns	22
Hens in the garden	23
What do you know about chicken biology?	24
Mrs Stayput and Vicious Vera	26
Clever hens	28
Queeny and Henrietta	29
Cockerels and fertilising eggs	30
The dangers of keeping a cockerel	31
Yum-Yum Corner: Advanced Egg Cooking	32
Boiling the perfect egg three different ways	32
What to do with eggshells	34
Fried eggs	34
Using up left-over boiled eggs	35
Research: Finding out about bread	38

3
MAKING A CHICKEN OUT OF AN EGG

Candling eggs	41
Hatching eggs	42
Incubating eggs	42
Checking out a broody hen	43
Facts about eggs	43
The battle of the rotten eggs	44
Yum-Yum Corner: Omelettes	47
All you need is egg and bread	49
Research: Finding out which chicken lays which egg	50
Egg identification	51

4
EGGS AND BROODY HENS

Looking after the eggs	55
Eggs, more eggs and Labradors	55
Making a hen broody	56
Yum-Yum Corner: Custards, sweet or savoury	60
Quick sweet custard	60
Floating islands	61
Sweet custard and bread pudding	61
Sweet custard and bread and butter pudding	61
Sweet custard and French toast	62
Research: Finding out about custard tarts	62
The cracking eggs experiment	63
Custard pie fights	64

5
CHICKENS AS FOSTER MOTHERS

Learning about partridges	67
Back to the yard: being a foster mother to partridges	69
Fostering to ducklings	70
Yum-Yum Corner: Savoury custard	75
Blind pastry cases for custard tarts and quiches	76
Research: Savoury custards and quiche	78
Designer eggs for tea	78
Five Little Ducks	79

6
SEXING CHICKENS

That's not a pullet, it's a cockerel	82
Yum-Yum Corner: Using up strange-shaped eggs and blind cases	84
Custard Tart	84
Quiche (savoury custard tart)	84
Savoury tarts	84
Savoury custard and bacon and egg pie	85
Savoury custard and sausage tart	85
Research: Find out about shop-bought pastry	86
Experiments with pastry	87

7
BATTERY HENS AND EGGS

Making a new hen out of an old battery	91
The Christmas cockerel	94
Yum-Yum Corner: Chicken roast, the basic method	96
What to do with a broiler (boiling hen)	97
Fried chicken	97
Chicken pie	98
Lemon chicken - very fattening, yummy treat	99
Cooking your Christmas capon	100
Research: Finding out about which chickens you can buy	101
Experiment with blowing eggs	101

8
INDIAN RUNNERS

Naughty boys and spotty ducks	105
Duck eggs	106
Yum-Yum Corner: Roast duck	108
Crispy fried duck with pancakes	109
Research: Finding out about ducks for roasting	110
Experiment: observation of a duck pond	111
The Ugly Duckling	112

9

BECOMING A DUCK OWNER

Learning about ducks	116
Yum-Yum Corner: Roast duckling and orange sauce	119
Duck breast and new vegetables (an August feast)	120
Crispy duck legs and roast potatoes	121
Duck risotto	122
Mallard and other wild ducks	123
Devilled duck	123
Research: Finding out about potatoes for roasting	124

10

BARNEY AND THE GANDERS

Things to consider before cross-fostering	127
A very confused goose	127
Hatching across species	128
A broody goose	129
Barney's new mate	130
Learning about imprinting	131
Barney and George: love at last	132
The madness of a gander	133
Territorial behaviour	134
Yum-yum Corner: Cooking a goose and goose eggs	135
Roast goose	135
Research: Finding out about fat	136
Experiment: making lard and crackling	137
Goosey goosey gander	137

11

GUINEA FOWL AS GUARD DOGS

Learning about guinea fowl	139
Roald Dahl's pheasant poaching trick	141
Yum-Yum Corner: Roast guinea fowl and stuffing	142
Research: Finding out about bones and gravy	143
The bone experiment	143
The Guinea Fowl (poem)	144

Chapter One

Chickens and Me, sorry Chickens and I

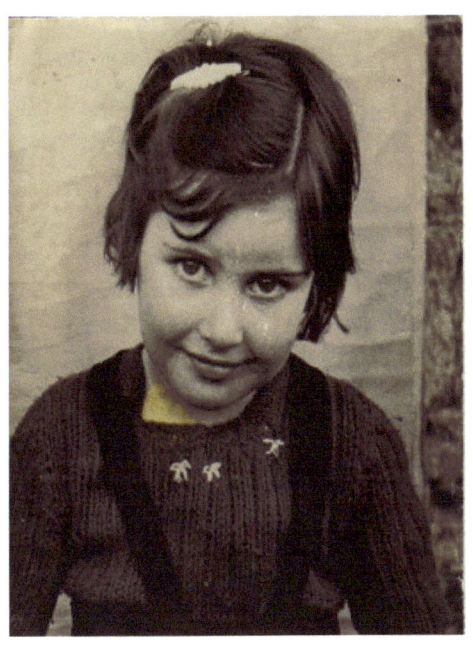

Dear Grandchildren…

Many, many years ago I met a chicken in the wood. My parents were squatting in a hut left behind in 'Underwood' by the Americans at the end of the war. It was large, with four rooms and a pot-bellied stove in the middle. There was a sink but no toilet – I think we used something called an Elsan to wee in. The hut had a round sloping roof stretching from wall to wall and covered in grass for camouflage. My sister and I would climb to the top of the roof and roly-poly down again. Fantastic!

A child in Underwood

The wood was an old broadleaf wood, no trees in straight lines or conifers. It was a working wood with woodmen always felling trees. This job was still done by hand with axes. No chainsaws then. The men would cut chips of wood out of the tree trunk until they had a large wedge or 'gob' removed. This gob had to face the very spot they wanted the tree to land on. They would then get each end of a huge saw and cut through to the gob. They

Chapter One

took it in turns to pull the saw through the tree. They never pushed, just pulled. So they went Pull and Rest, Pull and Rest, each man waiting his turn to pull hard. It never took very long before the shout of 'timber!' filled the air and the tree came crashing down.

My job was to watch without being seen and to report the spot to mother ASAP when the men had gone. There were quite a few families squatting in the huts and competition for everything was fierce. After telling her quietly, we would head out in the evening with sacks to gather the huge chips to fuel the pot-bellied stove. The Americans had been provided with coke to fuel the stoves. This gave out more heat and stayed alight longer. The remains of each fire, cinders, ash and clinker, were sprinkled on the pathways joining the huts and leading to the road out. This was another source of fuel for our stove. The pathways were dug up and sieved to find anything still burnable. As a result the pathways between huts soon became waterlogged. A quagmire in which to slither and slide through on our way to the main road.

Another source of free fuel was the train line. Father worked on the railway and would get the fireman on the train to drop off a bag of coal at the side of the line to be picked up later by mother and secreted in the pram, the area under the mattress and baby. Lots of things were hidden under babies during the war. Firemen in those days were not just the men in red fire engines; they were also the men who stoked the fires on trains to keep the steam engines running.

Something else mother would have us do was make little sandcastles with flowerpots and stand them to dry in the sun. The material used for this was black and quite powdery. We mixed it with stinky black stuff to make it stick together. I think it was probably slack and aviation fuel, but I can't be sure today. Good idea not to try this in the log burner. The scrub up after was painful.

We would gather other things from the wood too. Acorns and chestnuts were gathered in the autumn. These were dried and then put into sacks, and then we would bash them with a big old heavy pan to break them up. This was then used for hen food. The hens liked other things too, like hawthorn berries, elderberries and sycamore wings. Anything you see birds eating can be stolen from the hedgerows for the chickens. The rose hips however were not for chucks. They were taken to school, where the newly-formed National Health Service took them away and made rose hip syrup for babies. (There is a very old recipe for rose hip syrup at the end of this chapter. It is yummy!)

Most of my days were free to explore the woods and play as I wished. I was a very happy little girl, a child of the woods. I remember wandering all day picking berries and nuts. It was of course always sunny, always quiet and I was always alone. One sunny afternoon was spent lying on my tummy in the grass. I was picking and eating tiny strawberries, the most delicious strawberries I ever ate. You can sometimes buy wild strawberries today, but I'm sure the taste is not so intense.

Alone but not lonely

Being alone is a strange concept. I was never lonely as a child, but I was alone with the deer, frogs and snakes, butterflies and bees, rabbits and squirrels, stoats and weasels, foxes and badgers. Wow, squirrels were red in those days.

Sometimes the hunt came through. I was trained to run home quickly when I heard the noise of the hunting horn. The wood would be filled with the screaming and baying, shouting and howling of hounds. The noise was awesome. The pounding hooves in their careless gallop filled me with dread. It made my heart pound and made me sick. When they were gone the wood was silent for a long, long time. Very slowly everybody came out of hiding and the little sounds of chirruping bird and rustling hedgehogs would begin again. I hated the hunt.

Meeting Chucky

Alone and quiet is what I was as a little girl. We were the generation who were seen but not heard. I had learnt that this went for outside as well. If I walked or sat quietly, birds and animals would come near. It was the very opposite of the hunt. Some of them would even come up to me if I was very still and offered reward.

Chapter One

My favourite was an old hen. I met her one day whilst picking blackberries. I froze when I saw her and stood very still. She watched me and I watched her. She was beautiful, deep red brown with shiny dark eyes and a bold red comb on her head. I gently threw a blackberry to her. It took time, but she slowly pecked it up. I threw another. She was brave and came close, soon waiting for me to throw another berry. I sat slowly down because the berries were nearly gone and I hoped she would not run away when I stopped feeding her. Soon she was next to me, eating quickly. Chickens don't chew their food so it wasn't long before they were all gone.

She looked at me, tipping her head from side to side as if trying to focus on me. She began to talk to me whilst she turned over the leaves with her feet. Her 'chuck, chuck' sounded more like 'chawk'. Sometimes she sounded like she had put an L in it – clawk, clawk. So she talked to me as she raked about the ground with her feet. Big slow movements, first right and then left, head down and bottom up, scattering leaves and uncovering tasty morsels.

I now found out that she liked to eat other things, and I was not happy to see her pull up an enormous long red worm and eventually swallow it. It took some doing. She waved it back and forth and bashed it up and down all the time, making a little more of it disappear down her neck. Clawk, clawk again, scrape scrape. My new friend. Chucky.

Many years later I found that 'clawk, clawk, clawk' was how mother hens call the chicks to eat when they have found something good. So Chucky was actually calling me to lunch. Was I really supposed to share her worm as I had shared my berries?

I never told anyone about Chucky, because I had seen what my mother could do to a chicken with the kindling axe. She had once earmarked a big old cockerel to cook for tea but couldn't ring its neck. Holding him by the legs, she carted him off to the chopping block outside the woodshed. She swiftly threw him across the block and chopped off his head with the kindling axe. It was over in a second. She let go his legs and he took off across the yard whilst the nerves in his body reacted to the freedom. This only lasted a second I am sure, but it seemed an age to me. This was also one of the funniest things I can remember. I'm sure we shouldn't laugh, but sometimes the most gruesome things can be very, very funny, like when Granny fell over in the snow and we all saw her heavy-duty knickers.

I liked the chickens in the yard and the eggs they gave every day. I liked the little chicks they hatched sometimes. I never let myself love them as I loved Chucky. You never knew which of them would be in the next chicken pie you had to eat for dinner. My worst moments came when I heard mother shout 'come and help me choose a hen for tea'. I could never, never choose. Even the miserable old girl who pecked my legs when I was sent to collect eggs made me sad when she was eventually the chosen one. It was almost always the oldest, scruffiest looking one that was past laying eggs that was chosen for the pot. These are called broilers. Rid yourself of the image of tender white chicken breast roasted and succulent you are served for lunch these days. These old broilers were tough, usually boiled with dark flesh and tasting rank. They were impossible to chew with the milk teeth of a four-year-old. The only good thing was that the gravy made the potatoes taste good. A broiler hen would feed the entire family for a week. The potatoes, like the coal, appeared from under the baby in her pram. I don't remember how they got there. I'll share some recipes for old broilers with you later, but I don't expect you will be able to find one in the supermarket.

Becoming eggbound

When I was much older I went to stay with Auntie Jessamine (pronounced with esses not zeds, she would get very irate if you called her Jezzamine). I was about nine. Her hens were kept in a pen. They were not free to walk about and scratch for food like Chucky did. Their yard was bare earth with little to occupy them and unlike our hens in the yard they were shut in. They were nasty to each other. They were fed corn and layers' mash on a daily basis. This rich diet

Chapter One

made them quarrelsome and energetic, like hyperactive children. Since they didn't have to work for their food they spent most of their time chasing each other around, pecking at each other's bum feathers. Feather pecking is cruel and can end up as cannibalism. Peck, Peck, Peck! These hens talked a very different language. Squawk, squawk! Screech, screech! Carge, carge! Kult, kult! All these words are hen swear words, and you mustn't use them in the playground.

These hens chased and argued all day. Those that weren't fast enough were pecked, not just feather pecked but whole lumps of bum were pecked out. Feather pecking is chicken bullying and like bullying at school, it often goes too far.

One day Auntie made me hold a hen still at the old kitchen table whilst she stitched its parson's nose back on. Finding what she needed in the table drawer, she stitched away with ordinary needle and thread. It calmly sat there and let her do it. Chickens do this, if you gently put your hands over their eyes and hold them very still. Sometimes you can put them down on the floor and they still remain mesmerised. This one hardly needed holding at all. When the job was done Auntie smeared its rear end with some tar-like stuff and turned it loose. I remember wondering how on earth it would lay an egg through that job as it staggered away with its stitched-up bald bum covered in pitch.

Having an egg stuck can kill a hen. It's called being eggbound. Some people get egg bound when they can't say what they think and keep it all inside. They get a very red face and fume and fuss and throw their weight about. They are very unpleasant to be with, like a constipated baby.

My father, your great-grandfather, was often eggbound. So was one of my teachers, called Mr Farr. He used to keep it under control by thwacking his leg with his switch as he prowled up and down the rows between our desks. Sometimes, of course, hitting himself didn't suffice, so he had to thwack one of us instead.

Sometimes he thwacked when he wasn't eggbound. We were told to paint a picture from nature. He pinned a picture of a tiger on the board. I had never seen a tiger. My favourite natural thing was Chucky, so I painted her. Beautiful copper red with a piercing black eye and glorious red comb; the picture filled my page. My friends had all painted the tiger, lots of yellow and black stripes and green undergrowth for camouflage. Mr Farr walked the aisles offering comments and criticisms here and there. He stopped at my desk and bellowed 'what is this?' I was incensed. Anyone could see it was my beautiful chucky. 'It's a hen,' I announced in a tone of voice that implied he must be blind. That's when I found out how to make a grown man eggbound.

Chickens and Gamekeepers

I didn't really have much to do with hens when we left Underwood to live in the town. When I was grown up with children of my own I found myself needing to get to know chickens again. I was married to a gamekeeper and so became a keeper's wife. Gamekeepers look after game birds like pheasants and partridges all through the summer so that posh folk can shoot them in the winter.

Chickens are a major part in the rearing of pheasants and partridges.

Cock pheasants are beautiful birds, very bright and colourful. Each cock has several wives and should therefore

Chickens play a major part in the rearing of pheasants and partridges.

A Cock Pheasant

A Hen Pheasant

Chapter One

have lots of babies. Hen pheasants are very dull coloured and well camouflaged. They are also very dull brained, in fact you might want to call them stupid if you wanted to be rude. Hen pheasants make their nests, just scrapes in the ground, in the most ridiculous places sometimes, such as on the side of the road or down beside a gatepost. Often it's somewhere where they could be seen by humans and sniffed out by foxes. Both humans and foxes eat pheasants. Sometimes humans gather up the eggs while the hen has gone off for food and water, thinking they have been deserted. They kindly take the eggs to the gamekeeper, who is furious at their lack of understanding, but says nothing.

Pheasants are good at laying eggs but sometimes forget where they have laid them. Sometimes they start to brood the eggs (that means keep them warm so they will hatch), only to lose interest and start to lay another clutch of eggs somewhere else. When the baby pheasants hatch, hen pheasants often lose them. They cannot count. So as long as they can hear 'peep, peep, peep,' behind them, they keep on walking. They wander off and leave the chicks behind. These poor little things soon get cold and die, or are eaten by predators.

Mother hens on the other hand are fantastic at hatching eggs. They are brilliant at keeping babies warm and they call loudly all the time so that chicks know where they are. They are also a bit dim, because they cannot tell their own eggs from those of a pheasant or partridge. This is how gamekeepers can fool them into rearing pheasants instead of chickens.

Back in the 60s and 70s when your parents were young, most pheasants were hatched under chickens. Each chicken would have her own little house with a little grass run for the chicks to exercise in and learn to catch insects. There would be rows and rows of these coops on the rearing field. All of these houses would be moved every day and the birds all fed and watered. They also had to be guarded from foxes and other predators like cats, stoats, weasels and rats. This was Keeper's job.

Keeper's wife looked after the hens in the yard. These were not busy with game birds. Some of them would be crafty and not go broody in the nest boxes where they would be whisked off by Keeper to hatch more pheasants. They would find their own place to brood a clutch and appear out of the woods with a brood of chicks. This kept a continual stock of new hens and warm bottoms to put eggs under.

I found out all sorts of facts about chickens that will help you if you ever want to keep them yourself.

What do you know about poultry?

'Poultry' is the word used for all birds in the yard, like chickens, ducks and geese. All female poultry lay eggs. There are two main uses for eggs. One is to eat them and the other is to hatch them into new poultry. There are three main types of eggs we can buy to eat in Britain. Chicken eggs you can buy these almost everywhere. Duck eggs are becoming easier to buy, but usually only in the early summer. Goose eggs are hard to find, but you can sometimes buy them at poultry markets in the spring. All these eggs are different sizes and take different times to boil. They also need different sized eggcups. Ordinary eggcups are hens' egg size. For duck eggs you need something bigger than an egg cup, a wine glass maybe. For the massive goose egg you need something really big, like a jam jar or a coffee mug.

Chickens and their eggs

Chickens come in all different shapes and sizes. Big ones are called chickens and small ones are called bantams. Big chickens lay big eggs. One type of chicken is called Isa Brown, a big brown hen who lays big brown eggs. If you keep her happy she will lay you an egg almost every day for a whole year. Another big hen is called Welsomer. Her eggs are the most beautiful and the darkest brown you will ever find, unless you meet a Maran. They are also very big. She doesn't like the winter though and will not give you any eggs when it is cold.

Small chickens of course lay small eggs. One type of small chicken is called a silky bantam. She is a little

Chapter One

Isla Brown

Welsomer Eggs

Silky Bantam

soft fluffy hen who lays very small white or blue eggs. She loves sitting on eggs to hatch them.

Yum-Yum Corner
Learning to cook eggs

You can eat all types of eggs, even crocodiles' eggs. You can eat them raw and you can eat them cooked. How you cook them and for how long depends on the type of egg. We are going to use hens' eggs as our baseline and change the cooking times and methods according to size and species.

We often say 'they can't even boil an egg' when we talk about someone who can't cook. This leads us to think that boiling an egg is easy. In fact it is quite difficult to get the perfect boiled egg, one which has a yellow yolk for dippy bread but no trace of runny white. There are many things that can change the perfection of your boiled egg. For instance whether or not your egg has been in the fridge and is very cold. So rule number one, never keep eggs in the fridge. Secondly, the age of your egg can make a difference to the quality of your boiled egg. Second rule, always use very fresh eggs if you want a dippy egg, but never use a fresh egg for hard-boiled eggs because you can't get the shell off. Thirdly, the type of egg and the diet of the bird make a big difference, because the shell thickness varies. If chickens don't get enough grit in their diet the shell of the egg is quite thin and soft, so they don't need as much cooking time. If the egg has been laid by a goose or a guinea fowl, the shell will be thick and the egg will need longer to have that perfect dippiness. The final rule then is to be prepared to experiment and get to know your eggs with practice. It's a good idea to keep the menu to yourself and announce what is for tea when you have seen how your eggs have turned out.

Chapter One

4 ways to Cook Very Fresh Eggs for Tea

1 Boiling

Fill a pan with water and bring it to the boil. Put your eggs in very gently with a spoon – if you drop them in, the shell will crack and the water will get in and spoil your egg. Cold eggs will stop the water boiling. When the water comes to the boil again start the timer. You need to gently boil the eggs for 3 minutes if you want them runny for dipping soldiers. If you rapidly boil the eggs they will be buffeted about and get little cracks in the shell that will let in water.

Different-sized eggs need different amounts of cooking. Little bantam eggs will need a minute less and big old goose eggs will need a good 7 minutes. You can test to see if they are cooked the way you want them before you cut the top off. Firstly, the shells of eggs that are cooked will dry very quickly when you take them out of the water. Another thing you can do is sit the egg in an egg cup and use the tip of a very sharp knife to make a tiny pin hole in the shell. If the egg white oozes out you need to pop it back in the water for a minute. If nothing oozes, make the hole a little bigger to be sure the white is cooked to some depth.

2. Poaching

Boil some water in a pan and add a little vinegar. White vinegar is best.

Crack a very fresh egg into a cup. When the water boils, turn down the heat and swirl the water round with a whisk. When you have a whirlpool in the water, gently pour the egg into the middle. Now turn off the heat and put on the pan lid. Leave the egg in the water for a minute or three until the white is just hard enough to lift the egg out whole with a slotted spoon. If you cool the egg down quickly you can keep the egg like this for a long time. If you have lots of people you can get each egg ready like this and keep them somewhere cool. Some people put them into iced water to be sure they have stopped cooking. If you keep them warm they will keep cooking and be hard when you eat them. When you are ready to eat, just pop all the eggs into some hot water for half a minute and they will all be perfect at the same time.

3 Scrambling

Scrambled eggs make a terrible mess of the pan. If you don't have a non-stick pan, best use the microwave method. Crack as many eggs as you want to use into a basin and beat until no separate bits of white or yolk show. I use two for each person. Heat some butter in a non-stick pan on a gentle heat and pour the eggs in. Stir the eggs all the time until they are

Chapter One

almost cooked. Take off the heat while they are a little bit runny, because they keep on cooking while they are still in the pan. Spoon out onto your toast and put the pan in soak so it won't be hard to wash up.

If you microwave them, do it in short blasts and stir them every 30 seconds. All microwaves are different, so you will need to experiment with yours. They will also keep cooking when you take them out, so best to stop cooking when they're a little runny.

You can add all sorts of things to your eggs to make them delicious. Salt and pepper is a must, chives are delicious and so are little bits of bacon. You should experiment and see what you like. You can also add milk or cream if you want your eggs softer and runnier. My favourite is quite runny with beans on toast.

4 Frying

Gently heat lots of butter in a frying pan. Crack in your eggs, turn the heat right down and leave in the hot butter until they will lift out without breaking and the white is solid.

Horror! This is what most people do: Heat some oil in a very hot frying pan. When it is smoking hot crack in your eggs and watch them blister. When the egg bottoms are brown and

crunchy flip the eggs over and cook until you match the brown crunchiness on both sides. Rescue from the pan just as it begins to smoke. Barbaric, isn't it?

Finding out about shop bought eggs

Next time you go to the supermarket with the children, take your research note book with you. Take a good look at the eggs.

How many different kinds of eggs do they have?

How many different sizes of eggs do they have?

What are they called?

What is the difference between ordinary eggs, 'red tractor' eggs and RSPCA eggs?

Which eggs would you buy?

Chapter One

Fresh Eggs Experiment

If you are not sure how fresh your egg is, fill a glass with cool water and gently drop in the egg. If it floats it is fresh. If it sinks it is old and still OK to eat, but it won't taste as good.

If you have lots of fresh eggs, you could carry out an experiment to see how you prefer your eggs. I like 3 minutes for dipping, 6 minutes for salad and sandwiches and 7 minutes for grating into sauces. You will need 4 eggs, 4 egg cups and a pan of boiling water. Put 4 eggs into your water and wait until the water comes back to the boil. Start the timer. Take one out at 3 minutes and pop it into an egg cup. One minute later, take out the second for a 4-minute egg. Keep going until you have 5-minute and 6-minute eggs. Now cut the tops off and see which is your favourite. Which one is the easiest to take the shell off? Write down your results in a notebook.

Rosehip syrup

Rosehips contain twenty times more vitamin C than oranges. During World Ward 2, people were provided with a recipe by the government to make rosehip syrup for their children. After the introduction of the health service, mothers were given it free for their babies

This rosehip syrup recipe is made from hips from the hedgerow. It can be a drink watered down like squash, or it can be used as a syrup, like maple syrup, on pancakes and things. It's not bad in vodka if Nan fancies a little cocktail!

Ingredients:

2 Pounds of rosehips. (Any rose will do, even the tiny dog roses.)
3 pints of water
Half a pound of dark brown soft sugar

Chapter One

Method

Bring to the boil 3 pints of water. Chop rosehips until quite small. (You could do this in a food processor in your modern kitchen – mother would have spent a lot of time chopping.) When the rosehips are mashed, add to the boiling water. Bring water back to the boil, then remove from heat and allow to steep (that means soak to get the flavour out) for 20 minutes.

Pour rosehips and liquid into a clean jelly bag, tie it up and hang it over a pan to catch the drips. Let it drip for 24 hours. If you don't have a jelly bag an old, clean pillow case will do (make sure there is no fluff in the corners though). When the dripping has stopped, put the liquid in a saucepan and add the sugar. Bring to the boil and let it simmer for 5 minutes. Pour into sterilized bottles and seal. It will keep the whole winter if you have been very clean and the bottles were sterile.

Mother used to turn a kitchen chair up onto another chair so the four legs were available to tie string round. She would then put the old jam bowl on the unturned seat and tie the jelly bag/pillow case to the feet of the chair and leave it to drip. Woe betide anyone who knocked against it and clouded the liquid!

Chicken Little

"How do you know, Turkey Lurkey?"

"Henny Penny told me."

"How do you know, Henny Penny?"

"Chicken Little told me."

"How do you know, Chicken Little?"

"I saw it with my eyes. I heard it with my ears. Some of it fell on my tail."

Foxy Loxy said, "We will run. We will run into my den, and I will tell the king."

They ran into Foxy Loxy's den, but they did not come out again!

Chicken Little was in the woods. An acorn fell on his tail. Chicken Little said, "The sky is falling. I will run."

Chicken Little met Henny Penny. He said, "The sky is falling, Henny Penny."

Henny Penny said, "How do you know, Chicken Little?"

"I saw it with my eyes. I heard it with my ears. Some of it fell on my tail."

"We will run," said Henny Penny." "We will run and tell the king."

They met Turkey Lurkey. Henny Penny said, "The sky is falling, Turkey Lurkey."

"How do you know, Henny Penny?"

"Chicken Little told me."

"How do you know, Chicken Little?"

"I saw it with my eyes. I heard it with my ears. Some of it fell on my tail."

Turkey Lurkey said, "We will run. We will run and tell the king."

They met Ducky Lucky. Turkey Lurkey said, "The sky is falling, Ducky Lucky."

"How do you know, Turkey Lurkey?"

"Henny Penny told me."

Chapter One

"How do you know, Henny Penny?"

"Chicken Little told me."

"How do you know, Chicken Little?"

"I saw it with my eyes. I heard it with my ears. Some of it fell on my tail."

Ducky Lucky said, "We will run. We will run and tell the king."

They met Goosey Loosey. Ducky Lucky said, "The sky is falling, Goosey Loosey."

"How do you know, Ducky Lucky?"

"Turkey Lurkey told me."

"How do you know, Turkey Lurkey?"

"Henny Penny told me."

"How do you know, Henny Penny?"

"Chicken Little told me."

"How do you know, Chicken Little?"

"I saw it with my eyes. I heard it with my ears. Some of it fell on my tail."

Goosey Loosey said, "We will run. We will run and tell the king."

They met Foxy Loxy. Goosey Loosey said, "The sky is falling, Foxy Loxy."

"How do you know, Goosey Loosey?"

"Ducky Lucky told me."

"How do you know, Ducky Lucky?"

How do you know, Turkey Lurkey?"

"Henny Penny told me."

"How do you know, Henny Penny?"

"Chicken Little told me."

"How do you know, Chicken Little?"

"I saw it with my eyes. I heard it with my ears. Some of it fell on my tail."

Foxy Loxy said, "We will run. We will run into my den, and I will tell the king."

They ran into Foxy Loxy's den, but they did not come out again!

Chapter Two

Life in the Yard

Chapter Two

Finding out about free-range hens and bantams

Free range hens are free to wander around, usually in a field. They like to eat grass and worms and insects. Their diet is rich in minerals and vitamins. They scratch about in the grass with very sharp toes and like to sprint about very fast when the mood takes them. Because of this they need lots of space. They are very bad for small gardens because they scratch up all the flowers and eat all the vegetables. They have very good eyesight and they can even pick blackberries. If you provide them with comfy nest boxes they will prefer to lay eggs in there than out in the open field. Or you can make little wigwams out of twigs and things in the corners or the field and under bushes and things.

Because of all the rich food free-range hens find, their eggs are the very best. The shells are hard and the yolks bright yellow. If you fry a free-range egg the yolk will stand to attention and almost peep over the side of the frying pan. It will also be delicious.

Hens in barns

Barn-laid eggs sound good and countrified. However, laying hens in barns have very little space to move around and are very overcrowded. The barns are often huge places with hundreds of hens. They have restricted space and little access to fresh air and fresh food. They peck each other and squabble over everything. They also do not have a sex life. No point in feeding a cockerel when you don't intend to hatch the eggs. They have places to lay their eggs but not usually comfy nest boxes. Hens take less time to lay an egg if they are not made comfy, and bare boxes are easier to clean.

There is a huge variety of hens.

Sebright   Jersey Giant

They range from tiny bantams like Sebrights to huge great birds like the Jersey Giant, which can weigh 10 pounds. Sebrights weigh about 20 ounces, tiny indeed and very good-natured. Their eggs are no bigger than 20p pieces. These are special because the male and female have the same feathers. Very beautiful. You can only tell the male when he grows his comb.

The Jersey Giant does not have a lot to recommend it as the breed of choice for the gamekeeper's yard. The hens are big with clumsy great feet, and they don't lay many eggs. They eat a lot, give you few eggs and not good broody hens. But they are very sweet tempered, both cockerels and hens, and they put up with being picked up and cuddled, so if you want a pet chicken, this is the one for you.

Hens in the garden

If you are thinking of getting hens, you will have great fun researching the breed you want online. Make a list of what you want from your hens and check out the qualities of different birds. There are dozens to choose from. Some are very beautiful, whilst others are plain. Some are passive and cuddly, whilst others are vicious and nasty. You can also go to a poultry show, where owners proudly display their hens like other people show dogs and cats. It's a great day out and you can often buy your hens or place an order. People usually start with a trio – one cockerel and two hens. If you have close neighbours you might want to be considerate and not get a cockerel. They are noisy little brutes, specially at daybreak and every time they mate with a hen, it's 'cock-a-doodle-doo!'

The first thing to decide is whether you want free range hens, barn hens or back yard birds. If you encourage them into the house and garden they will be disrespectful and difficult to keep safe. They are happiest if they can roam free, but they peck everything and poo everywhere.

What do you know about chicken biology?

It might be useful here to tell you a little about chicken biology. You know already that chickens don't have teeth and that they swallow food whole. In front of their neck they have a thing called a crop under the skin. This is like a purse or pocket where the food first goes. If a chicken eats a lot you can see it swelling, so it must be very elastic. It's very funny to watch them filling their crops under the oak tree eating acorns as they fall from the tree. Get a man to make a fist, and that is how big a crop can grow. It holds a fair few acorns.

Chickens will persevere for a long time to get what they find down their necks and into their crops. One old hen leapt onto a rubber band disregarded by the postman. It looked very like a worm to her beady eye. Keeper's wife (that's me) was hanging out washing and saw her pick it up. The hen tried to arrange the thing for swallowing it in her beak, throwing her head back and forth, up and down, side to side. She couldn't get it down. What she succeeded in doing was curling the thing around her beak until she couldn't open it.

By now Keeper's wife was laughing so much she could barely pick up the pegs. The whole thing got even funnier when the chicken got her little sharp inner toe caught in the rubber band as she tried to dislodge the thing with her foot. Down came her head as she pulled on the rubber band. Up went her head as she released the pressure. Up, down, up, down, up, down. She looked like she was saluting the Queen at the Changing of the Guard.

When she tired of her efforts and sat still for a while and Keeper's wife had finished laughing, the rubber band was easily removed. The story was told to the postman with good humour, which meant he never threw away rubber bands again in our yard. It's always best to complain to someone in the nicest possible way. That way things can get fixed.

Gizzards

From the crop the food passes to the chicken's gizzard. This is often opened out flat and cleaned in the giblets of an oven-ready bird you buy at Christmas. Lots of creatures, like dinosaurs, crocodiles and alligators, have gizzards instead of teeth. It is a specialised stomach, sometimes called a 'gastric mill' because it is a stomach that grinds up food like a mill grinds up flour. It has thick muscular walls that contract and squeeze to grind up food as it passes through. To help this happen, chickens swallow little stones and bits of grit. That way the gizzard works a bit like a pestle and mortar and grinds the food small enough to continue through the intestines.

Because of the need to supply the gizzard with grit, chickens often eat stupid things like bits of glass, snail shells and pebbles. You can buy grit for your chickens that is just right for them.

Back to the Yard

There was once a beautiful Lavender Muscovy duck in the yard. She hung around the garage a lot, probably because she could keep an eye on the pond from there. Over the course of a week she got thinner and thinner. Keeper's wife found her dead one morning and took the body to Keeper. He was always on the alert for any possible disease in the yard, so he carried out a post mortem. He found her gizzard full of nuts and bolts. This was not as easily fixed as the rubber band episode. The moral of the tale is,

Chapter Two

if you are going to let your chickens roam free you need to tidy away things that they may eat.

Mrs Stayput and Vicious Vera

The hens in our yard were a mix of different breeds. They all looked different and had different temperaments. These personality traits often led to their names. Several hens made names for themselves, although we never named them all. Mrs Stayput was just that. She was a fabulous back yard bird. She would forage all day and rarely needed extra food in the summer. She started laying at four months and laid at least four eggs a week thereafter. She was a sucker for a cuddle and firm favourite of Littlest Son.

One day Keeper's wife found Littlest Son gently standing Mrs Stayput on the bonnet of his pedal car. She asked him what he was doing. 'You can pick her up and put her anywhere. She won't move,' he explained. Mrs Stayput did indeed just sit there. 'She likes a cuddle too,' he said, picking her up to demonstrate.

Vicious Vera, on the other hand, was not to be messed with. Even the best-bred hens can be vicious sometimes, especially when they have chicks with them. Most of the yard

Vicious Vera

Mrs Stayput

hens could feed themselves in good weather. Some are ferocious foragers and will tear through you garden and rip it to shreds. Some are more angry than others. They certainly don't like to be picked up and petted. They are always trouble and often come to a sticky end. When Keeper's wife called them to feed last thing at night so she could lock them safely away, Vicious Vera would hang back. 'Chuck, chuck, chuck' called Keeper's wife. 'Chuck away' came the reply as they all bundled back into the hen pen.

Not Vicious Vera. She would wait until you were leaving the pen and fly at your legs. Even if you were wearing wellies she could get up high enough to find flesh to peck, even through your trousers. When it was time to lock the hens up for the night she would leg it when she saw you coming. She would screech up and down the yard, avoiding the open hen house door at all costs. She made everyone else in the yard jittery. Concentrating on the well-behaved hens in the yard, Keeper's wife got them all in safe from the foxes and cats and closed their little hen flap door. Vicious Vera was lurking around the gate, waiting to offer her last spiteful peck of the day. Very frustrated, Keeper's wife skirted around her, leaving her to the dangers of the night. Was she secretly hoping that Vicious Vera would be fox food by morning?

She was still there in the morning, hanging around the nest boxes. Thinking she wanted to lay an egg, Keeper's wife opened up the nest boxes before letting the hens out and throwing them a scoop of corn. As the birds fed, she checked the nest boxes for eggs and there was Vicious Vera eating one. Yes. Not laying an egg but eating an egg! Cannibalism is a very big sin for a chicken. Death sentence for Vera the vicious one, I think.

Some hens are cleverer than others. These are the ones who suss out new things like unusual food. They will spot the nest of flying ants just hatching, or the row of freshly-sown radishes that have appeared as green delicacies overnight. Frog spawn tends to hatch into tadpoles or become baby frogs all at the same time. The result is a simultaneous appearance of tiny frogs leaving the pond and heading for cover in the

Chapter Two

woods. In the bible this would be called a plague of frogs. They are so cute, about as big as the end of your thumb and very jumpy. Henny Hawkeye was on the case the morning this happened. She squawked an alert to the rest of the girls and they were there in an instant. Boy did they have fun, dashing back and forth along the pond bank waiting for another batch of baby frogs. The bank was very steep and muddy and hens don't go in for swimming. They were hysterical as they held their balance trying to catch another tasty morsel, trying not to fall in, trying to fight off the other hens. Pushing and shoving like old ladies at the January sales.

Hysterical is probably the word to describe the daughter of the house as she pleaded with Keeper's wife to stop the carnage, tears and other stuff running down her face, very upset. That's why frogs have so many babies, Keeper's wife tried to explain. They are really nature's way of feeding other things. Daughter wasn't convinced that this was a good thing.

Clever hens

The clever hens are the ones who start the trouble. They are the ones who discover they can roost in a yew tree instead of being locked away in the shed, safe from foxes and out of the wind. Keeper's Land Rover was always parked under the tree at night and always covered in chicken poo in the morning. These are the hens who find places where they shouldn't go, like the newly planted out greenhouse. They perch on the five-bar gate, keeping order in the yard and of course producing a row of poo for folk to walk through when they visit. These hens are top of the pecking order. They rule the roost and boss all the other hens about. Usually they are pretty fierce, with a mean peck and a watchful beady eye. Anyone gets out of line and they are in trouble, and feathers fly as they dash around picking on anyone in the way. They are bullies. I've know some women who ruled their 'feathered pecked' husbands and children in the same way.

One spring an exceptionally big chick hatched. By autumn, she was massive. She was a lively, food-centred girl and she quickly became very humanized. Keeper's wife would chuck, chuck her and she would chuck, chuck back. She was happy to help hang out washing or sweep the yard. Her favourite job was helping to mow the grass – loads of yum yums flying off the mower. Usually, humanized hens were picked upon by the rest of the crew and treated with scorn. She, however, quickly became top hen in the yard, but still a very cuddly chicken. She ruled the roost with calm command and never bullied but gently persuaded the other hens to go where she wanted and do as she did. She became known as Queeny. She was never mean or threatening, but the others all respected her. She was no bully but a perfect role model for Keeper's wife.

Queeny and Henrietta

Funny thing is, although she was part of the yard, she never, never roosted next to any of the others. She slept alone on her perch. One winter's morning Keeper's wife found her hanging upside down on the perch she had used all her life with her wings spread out and her head in the dirt, dead as a dodo.

One day in March, Keeper's boy was given a hen for his birthday. She was a point of lay pullet. She had a little cage without a bottom so that she could eat grass and insects but could not do naughty things in the garden or get eaten by foxes. Each day the little cage was moved so that she had a new patch of grass.

The little boy loved his hen and called her Henrietta. At night he took her to his room, where she roosted on top of his wardrobe. One morning before the boy woke up, she was bursting to lay her first egg. She clucked and clucked around the bedroom looking for a nest box. She tried in the wardrobe, but there were too many shoes in the bottom to get comfortable. She went downstairs and looked around for a place to lay her egg. She flew up onto the sofa. She flew up onto the television. Everywhere she tried she pooed of course, making things even more slippery and lumpy.

Eventually she spotted the coal

Chapter Two

Queeny

Henrietta

bucket. The sides were high so she felt safe, and the lumpy bits of coal felt like eggs in there already. In short, it felt just like a well-used nest box.

Henrietta laid her first pearly white egg in amongst the black coal. It looked beautiful.

When Keeper's wife came downstairs to make a cup of tea she was very puzzled by the little black footprints on the stairs. She soon solved the puzzle when she went to make up the Rayburn and found the pearly white egg nestling in the coal. She thought it was time to make Henrietta a proper nest box and that maybe it was time for Henrietta to join the other hens in the yard. Hens don't really like to live with humans. They like another hen around to cluck at.

Cockerels and fertilising eggs

Cockerels contribute to life in the yard in two ways. They fertilise the eggs so that when mother hen sits on them little chicks grow and hatch. One cockerel can make eggs fertile for lots of hens and his work can make eggs fertile for up to a week at a time, so you don't need a cockerel

for every hen. Hens don't get jealous and don't mind sharing their mate with lots of friends.

Cockerels, however, do get jealous. If you have more than one cockerel they fight and squabble and won't let each other mate. A cockerel has to climb onto the hen's back to mate with her. If there are two cockerels they put each other off the business of mating and are knocked off the hen before her eggs are fertilized.

The other thing that cockerels do is to keep order. They will not stand for any bickering and squabbling in the yard. If they spot two of their hens having a fight they rush over and break it up, pecking the hens and squawking at them.

The dangers of keeping a cockerel

One day in April a new cockerel arrived in the yard. He was an Old English Game Cock. He was quite small, more like a bantam than a chicken, and very handsome with very bright plumage and a shiny red comb. He was also very spiteful. Pretty soon he was the boss of the yard and the big old cockerel hid from him. He strutted up and down the yard telling the hens off all day. He

pecked at chicks and ducks and geese and was altogether unpleasant.

One day Keeper's wife ran outside, hearing her small boy crying. The little red rooster was attacking the child and pecking his little fat legs. She asked Keeper to get rid of the cockerel, but he loved the little bird and didn't want to part with him.

One day, when Keeper was at the Game Fair, the wife came across the rooster taking a nap on a perch. She fetched a sack, grabbed the horrible bird by the legs and poked him into the sack. She then took him down the road to a friend who didn't have children to attack. I would like to say the rooster lived happily ever after, but I don't think he did.

Chapter Two

Yum-Yum Corner
Advanced Egg Cooking

Boiling the perfect egg three different ways

Method 1

Use a large pan and boil about 2 pints of water. The eggs need plenty of space. When the water is boiling gently lower the eggs into it, making sure you do not crack the shell. Put the lid on the pan and wait until the water is boiling again. Immediately turn down the heat and simmer very gently for 3 minutes. Take out each egg and allow it to rest in an egg cup for one minute and then crack the shell to let out the heat.

Method 2

Use a large pan and boil about 2 pints of water. The eggs need plenty of space. When the water is boiling gently lower the eggs into it making sure you do not crack the shell. Put the lid on the pan and wait until the water is boiling again. Boil for 5 seconds. Remove the pan from the heat and let it stand for 8 minutes if

you want soft boiled eggs, 12 minutes will give you a just moist yolk and 25 minutes will give the best hard-boiled eggs.

Method 3

Put cold eggs into cold water and heat to boiling. Boil for 5 seconds. Take off the heat and leave to stand for one minute for soft boiled eggs, 5 minutes for medium and 20 minutes for hard boiled. If you crack open your eggs and they have runny whites you can leave the rest a few more

minutes or you can scoop the lot out into a bowl, whisk with a fork and scramble them. If they are a perfect blend of set white and runny yolk you just have to serve with soldiers for dunking. If they are a little too set for dunking but not hard boiled, they are fantastic in a salad or kedgeree. If they are hard boiled then you need to put them with something moist like mayonnaise or cheese sauce.

Checking for dippiness

When you take an egg out of the water and put it in an egg cup it will dry because of the heat of the egg. If it only dries slowly you may have an underdone, sloppy egg. If you get the point of a very sharp knife and wriggle the tip just into the egg you may find some egg white leaks out. This means you have a sloppy white. Pop it back in for a bit longer. If no oozing white stick the knife in a little more. Still no leaky white then you have probably got the perfect dippy egg.

An experiment with soldiers

If they are a perfect blend of set white and runny yolk, you just have to serve with soldiers for dunking. Bread or toast for soldiers? This is a big, important decision. Get 2 slices of brown bread and 2 slices of white bread. These are best got from ready-sliced bread, because it is hard to cut fresh bread thin enough for soldiers. If you want to be very posh you can cut the crusts off the slices now. Butter one slice of white and one of brown and cut them into thin slices. Some people like them very long, the full width of the slice. These can be a fun dip with lots of wobbling. Most people cut the slices in half so they have more control over the dipping.

Toast the other two slices, butter and cut into your favourite shape. Some people put Marmite on toasted soldiers. Not sure how I feel about that. Now cook some eggs in your favourite way and see which soldiers you prefer.

Failing the dippy test

If you crack open your first egg and it has a runny white, you can leave the rest a few more minutes or you can scoop the lot out into a bowl, empty the shells and whisk with a fork to scramble them. If they are a little too set for dunking but not hard boiled, they are fantastic in a salad or kedgeree. If they are hard boiled then you need to put them with something moist like mayonnaise or cheese sauce because the yolks can be very dry.

What to do with eggshells

There are lots of old wives' tales about eggshells. Some people think you will get warts if you play with them. Some people think you should crush them up and put them into the chicken food, because they give the hen back the calcium she has used making the egg. Because they float some people think the fairies use them as boats. Uncle Paul says Elizabeth Fleming thinks the witches use them as boats to sail after the sailors and make their lives a misery. I have given you her poem at the end of this chapter. I hope you like it.

Fried eggs

I know, I said don't do it but there is just one exception:

Egg Top Hat

Take a slice of thick bread and cut a circle from the middle with a mug. Fry the slice and the piece you removed in hot sizzling butter. When brown turn over and then drop an egg into the hole. When the white is nearly set turn the whole thing to finish off the top. Serve on a plate with the round piece on top for the hat. Give it a smiley face with ketchup and see a boy smile as he tucks in.

Using up left-over boiled eggs

There are dozens of things you can do with left-over eggs, whether soft or hard boiled. Creamed eggs are the most versatile and are good on toast, in rolled-up pancakes, jacket potatoes or in sandwiches with cress.

Creamed eggs

Remove the eggs from the shell and place in a bowl. Mash the eggs thoroughly – a food processor is good for this if you have one. If they are very dry you can add a little cream or full-fat milk at this stage. You can now add anything that takes your fancy. Other leftovers like cold chicken or fish, crispy bacon or sausages. You can use any herbs or sauces you are fond of and any vegetables you have to hand. My personal favourite is grated cheese and ham. I spread it on toast and pop it under the grill. My least favourite is Marmite, but one of my kids loves this.

Scrambled eggs

Beat 6 eggs in a bowl with 2 tablespoons of cream. Place a non-stick pan over a low heat and pour in the eggs. Stir with a wooden spoon until the eggs are as set as you like them. There are no hard and fast rules about the consistency of scrambled egg, you choose, you're the chef. Now

flavour as you wish. Keep it simple with salt and pepper or go mad with anchovies, chives, cheese, or bacon. Just like every other way of cooking eggs, the world is your oyster once you have the basics. Oysters and scrambled eggs. Yum! Lots of people like them with smoked salmon.

Poached eggs

Here again you need to experiment with your own eggs to get the cooking time right, because we now know they are all different. Always use the freshest eggs for poaching. If you use old eggs you will get a flat egg that looks very tired. You do not need a poacher to make good poached eggs, you just need a wide shallow pan like a frying pan.

Method 1

Fill the frying pan with water to about an inch and a half and bring to the boil. Add a teaspoon of white vinegar. Crack each egg into a cup and gently slide it into the water. Turn down the heat so that you have a gently simmer. When the egg white looks solid, about 3 minutes, remove the egg with a fish slice and drain on paper towel.

Method 2

Fill the frying pan with water to about an inch and a half and bring to the boil. Add a teaspoon of white vinegar. Add a round pastry case.

Crack each egg into a cup and gently slide it into the water inside the pastry case. Turn down the heat so that you have a gentle simmer. When the egg white looks solid, about 3 minutes, remove the egg with a fish slice and drain on paper towel.

Method 3

Fill the frying pan with water to about an inch and a half and bring to the boil. Add a teaspoon of white vinegar. Keep the water boiling vigorously as you drop the cracked egg in from a height of about a foot. The shock of landing in boiling water will make the egg tuck itself into a very nice round ball. Turn down the heat and simmer for 3 minutes. Take out the eggs and drain on paper. This method is great if you want to make egg tartlets or to serve with smoked haddock.

Here again you need to experiment with your own eggs to get the cooking time right, because we now know they are all different. Always use the freshest eggs for poaching. If you use old eggs you will get a flat egg that looks very tired.

If you want you can buy an egg poaching pan that has individual cups for each egg and has boiling water below. These work quite well, but you need to practise. Put a little butter in the cups to stop the eggs sticking. Never boil the water and remember the eggs will keep cooking after you turn off the heat, so get them out of the cups ASAP. If you are worried about dropping eggs into water you can make them a little coat out of cling film. Cut off a fairly big bit of cling film and line a small cup with it, pushing it right down into the bottom. Crack your egg into the lined cup and draw the cling film up over the egg. Twist the cling film round and round and tie a knot it in so that the egg doesn't have any spare room. Get all the eggs you want ready and boil up a pan of water. Making sure the eggs have plenty of room place them in the boiling water. Turn the heat down really low and leave for 3 minutes.

Take one out and check it feels OK. If it feels very soft through the cling film then it needs longer. If it feels like squeezing a plump baby's arm then it is probably just right.

Chapter Two

Research
Finding out about bread

Next time you go to the supermarket with the children, take a research note book with you. Take a good look at the bread or bakery section. In the bread section/bakery look at all the different types of bread. See how some bread is white and some is brown.

How many types of white bread does your supermarket have?

How many types of brown bread does your supermarket have?

Are all the brown loaves the same shade of brown?

See how some bread is sliced and some is not. Are all the slices the same thickness?

Note down how many types of bread you think would be good for soldiers and dunking and explain why.

Conclusions

....

....

....

....

....

Eggshells

by Elizabeth Fleming (1934)

Oh, never leave your eggshells unbroken in the cup;
Think of us poor sailor-men and always smash them up,
For witches come and find them and sail away to sea,
And make a lot of misery for mariners like me.
They take them to the sea-shore and set them on the tide –
A broom-stick for a paddle is all they have to guide
And off they go to China or round the ports of Spain,
To try and keep our sailing ships from coming home again.
They call up all the tempests from Davy Jones's store,
And blow us into waters where we haven't been before;
And when the masts are falling in splinters on the wrecks,
The witches climb the rigging and dance upon the decks.
So never leave your egg-shells unbroken in the cup;
Think of us poor sailor-men and always smash them up;
For witches come and find them and sail away to sea,
And make a lot of misery for mariners like me.

Chapter Three

Making a chicken out of an egg

Making a chicken out of an egg

In the yard, the eggs laid by hens do not have chicks in. They are not fertile. If there is a cockerel in the yard, then there may be chicks in the eggs. You do not have to have a cockerel for every hen. Usually people keep about 5 or 6 hens to one cock.

How to tell if the egg is fertile or has a chick in it

When the egg is first laid you cannot tell if it is fertile and quite often they are not, especially at the beginning of the summer. If you are saving eggs to hatch under a hen or in an incubator, you need to choose and store the eggs very carefully. They need to be a perfect egg shape, with no hairline cracks. Cracks sometimes happen with big-footed hens. They also need to be clean. Hens sometimes forget where they are and do a poo in the nest box, and they never wash their feet. They also need to be turned over every day or the chick will stick to the inside of the shell and not be able to hatch properly.

Candling eggs

This is used to see if there is a chick

in the egg. By about 10 days the air sac should be big enough to see, if you carry out the experiment correctly. You will need a bright light, like a desk lamp, a cardboard tube like the inside of a toilet roll and two eggs, one that is fresh from the yard and another that has been sat on for about 10 days.

Candling eggs experiment

In a dark room, sit the fresh egg on the end of the tube and hold it in front of the light. What do you see? Now that you have had a practice, sit your fertile egg in the tube and do the same thing. You should now be able to see into the egg. Look at the round end of the egg. Is there an air sac? If you look very carefully you may see tiny blood vessels in the membrane and a tiny embryo. Usually you can only see the air sac, but that is a good indication that there is a chick in there. Get the egg quickly back under the hen, because if it gets cold the chick will die. Years ago people used a candle instead of a light, which is why we still call this candling eggs.

Hatching eggs

You can hatch any eggs in an incubator, even those of crocodiles. The instructions are pretty clear, but you can't just stick the eggs in and go away and wait. They need to be kept at the right temperature, turned over daily and kept moist with the correct humidity. Today you can buy incubators for as few as 12 eggs up to 1000s in big hatcheries. A hen's bum will work just as well if you haven't an incubator, with the added bonus that she will rear the chicks for you.

Incubating eggs

Keeping eggs warm to make the chick grow inside is called incubating them. When hens get the urge to incubate eggs they sit very tightly in the nest box. They are now called broody hens. If you slide your hand under a hen who does not want to get off the nest box you will find that her tummy is very, very warm. You may also get pecked, because she will think you are after her eggs. When they are not broody, hens don't mind you taking their eggs to eat. You see, there isn't a live chick in there until she begins to sit on them. So she may wait until she has laid twelve eggs before she starts to sit on them. It doesn't matter at this stage if the eggs get cold because the chick hasn't started yet. When she has laid enough eggs, a full clutch, she will start to sit on them.

Now is the time when the eggs have to be kept warm all of the time. If they get cold the chicks will die inside the shell. The broody hen still has to eat and drink. She has to be lifted off the eggs once a day and given food and water. At this time they usually do a very big smelly poo, so watch where you put your feet.

Checking out a broody hen

When a hen goes broody, she sits very tight on the eggs. If you slide you hand under her, palm upward, she will attempt to snuggle you in with the other eggs. It is as warm as toast in there and very cosy. Sometimes this will make her very angry and she will try to peck your hand off. If you leave the eggs and the number builds up to 10 or more the hen will get the urge to sit on them. If you want to keep collecting the eggs you can replace them with pot (fake) eggs, specially made for the job, or you can fool her with some golf balls. It's best not to leave her in the nest box where all the

other hens can disturb her. She should have her own safe nest box where she is safely shut in so that foxes can't eat her. This needs to be on the ground so there is natural humidity, but make sure there are no gaps where nasty creatures like rats can creep through and eat the eggs.

Facts about eggs

If you hard boil an egg, about 8 minutes, you will be able to see for yourself some of the things other people have never noticed. Take the shell off the egg. Do you see a very

Chapter Three

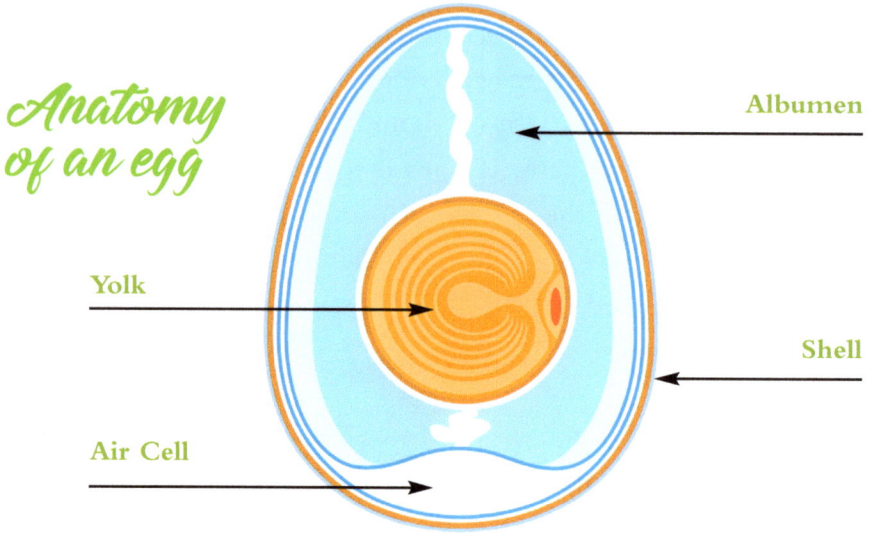

Anatomy of an egg

thin layer of skin that is quite hard to pinch off? If you take off all the shell you might have a dent in the top of the egg. This is the air sac. This air sac gets bigger as the chick grows inside the egg.

So you see there is more to an egg than meets the eye. The white is called the albumen and it forms around the fertilised egg. Its purpose is to protect the yolk and provide nutrition for the growth of the chick. The yolk is still inside the chick when it hatches and feeds it for a day or two whilst its little legs start to work and it can find food. I hope this information hasn't put you off your dippy egg for tea!

The battle of the rotten eggs

Years ago, especially during the war, people used to preserve eggs with stuff called isinglass. The eggs would all be put into a special wire bucket and lowered into the solution. Keeper used this old bucket or his hat for collecting pheasant eggs. When the pheasant eggs had all hatched and were snuggled up warm in the stable, the incubator had to be emptied and fumigated ready for next year. He used this same bucket to put all the unhatched eggs in while he cleaned.

Walking round the corner of the incubator shed with this bucket full of addled eggs, Keeper spotted two

Making a chicken out of an egg

teenage boys back from their job of feeding wild birds. He chose the most discoloured of the addled eggs and chucked it at them with full force. It exploded with a bang at the ground between their feet. They jumped in the air as the ghastly stink and gassy, farty air spread all around them. They felt sick. They soon realised that there was more to come and legged it into the wood, trying not to be sick. They ran in different directions. Keeper followed the bigger of the two, armed with the bucket of eggs.

The boy hid behind the huge old chestnut tree but left his bum sticking out behind. 'Thwack' went the second egg, right on the bottom. Trousers now steaming and stinking, the boy took off. The next one got him square between the shoulders. The next one landed in his ear. The slimy, sticky, stinking contents of the egg ran down his neck inside his shirt. He was grey now and trying hard not to be sick. By now Keeper was laughing so loud he could hardly get his aim but he still had a fair few eggs left in the bucket. The boy finally reached his bike that he left by the log store and pedalled off as fast as he could towards the rearing field.

Meanwhile the second boy had time to hatch a plan. Whilst Keeper was occupied with his mate, this boy remembered a clutch of well-rotted Muscovy duck eggs between the corn store and the stable. The gap was too small to easily gather the eggs and they had been left there for weeks to rot and fester. Some of them were a dark bottle green. He went to Keeper's shed and found a spoon which Keeper had bound to the end of a long stick. This home-made tool was for putting poison deep into rat holes. It worked perfectly for gathering the rotten eggs. Very, very carefully he put the eggs into an old flowerpot he found nearby. The job was just complete when his mate rode by on his bike.

Crashing to a halt, he joined his friend behind the wood shed and they set an ambush. Keeper still had half a dozen eggs left, but he misjudged his footing as he rounded the corner and leapt over a blue plastic bag in his path. His legs shot out from under him and he landed on his back. The remaining eggs in the bucket all exploded together, tainting Keeper's sleeve and arm. The fall meant he was no match for the 17 really rotten Muscovy eggs that were hurled at him. They got him from hat to boots. Every bit of him was covered in slimy, stinky, green mess.

When the fight was through and all eggy ammunition was used up, the bedraggled trio headed for the house. They were laughing and gagging and hanging on to each other. Best of friends now. There was evidence of the fight everywhere with bits of rotten egg hanging from shed doors and walls. The sight was gruesome and the stink hung over the cottage like a busted gas main.

They were in big trouble. Keeper's wife was furious as she headed them off in the yard. No way were they allowed in the house. She got the hose on the three of them and made them strip to their pants. Their clothes were disgusting. No washing machines in those days or showers and hot water. To take a bath they now had to light the Rayburn and wait for hot water. But even after the bath you could still smell rotten eggs. The whole place reeked, smelled like a gas leak for days.

Making a chicken out of an egg

Yum-Yum Corner
Omelettes

This is the time of year when there is a glut of eggs, so you can afford to make those recipes that are usually too expensive. Eggs are a useful source of protein, iodine and essential vitamins and help mothers to grow strong and healthy children. They are almost indispensable to the cook. Hens' eggs are the type of egg most frequently used in cooking. Duck eggs, gull eggs and quail eggs are less frequently used and are generally eaten on their own, rather than in baking. Pheasants' eggs are never available to people who don't rear the birds. Turkey eggs are also available to those working on the turkey farm and work just as well in all the recipes that call for eggs. I should say that we only eat the misshapen rejects. The boss wouldn't like it if we used up good eggs.

Chapter Three

Basic omelette

Beat 3 eggs in a bowl. Heat a non-stick pan on a very gentle heat. Pour in the eggs and wait for them to set. Roll the mixture up and slide onto a plate. You can add anything you like to the eggs as they cook. Salt and pepper of course. A big dollop of butter melted in the pan before you put the eggs in is good. Cheese and chives are my favourite. Watch out for things that might make the mixture wet, like tomatoes, as the omelette might not set before the bottom catches.

Plain omelettes

Beat 3 eggs in a bowl and season. Heat a small amount of fat or oil in a frying pan, being sure to cover the bottom of the pan. Pour in the eggs and turn down the heat. When the top starts to set, ease the omelette off the bottom of the pan so that it moves freely around. If you like you can now you can add anything you like to your omelette – bacon, mushrooms, spring onions, cooked vegetables etc. Then top with grated cheddar. When this melts, fold the omelette in half and serve with salad or chips.

Soufflé omelette

Chop, prepare and cook whatever you are going to add to your omelette. For a Spanish omelette you need a large Spanish onion, a red pepper, chorizo sausage and a very ripe tomato. Start off whatever you are going to add in the pan before you cook the omelette. Separate three egg whites from their yolks and beat the whites until they are stiff. Then gently fold in the yolks. Heat some fat in a pan and gently pour in the egg mixture or pour over your precooked ingredients. Cover with a lid and leave on a very low heat for 10 minutes. Remove the lid and add the cooked ingredients. Sprinkle with cheese and serve.

Spanish omelette

Begin by frying a large Spanish onion with a few chopped peppers and dried tomatoes. Using 3 eggs, separate the whites from the yolks and whisk the whites until you can turn the bowl upside down without them falling out. This is called 'stiff peaks'. Stir the yolks together and slowly and gently mix the whites and the eggs together. Slide them into a warmed non-stick pan on top of your cooked ingredients. Place the lid on the pan and wait for 5 minutes. The omelette is ready when the top is a little spongy and the bottom golden brown. Even better if you have some chorizo or paprika.

All you need is egg and bread
Eggy bread

Whisk 2 eggs in bowl until no bits of yolk or white show separately. Cut two thick slices of bread and take off the crusts. Keep the crusts for making breadcrumbs later. In a broad dish or plate soak the slices of bread in the egg. Make sure both sides are well soaked. Heat a non-stick frying pan on a low heat and put the slices in to cook. Turn and cook until both sides are golden brown. These can become sweet or savoury dishes. Add salt and pepper to make them delicious as part of a full English with crispy bacon and tomatoes. Add sugar and cinnamon, golden syrup or maple syrup to serve as a pudding with custard or serve with stewed fruit and cream, bananas or frozen fruit from last year. Jam or marmalade is also good for breakfast.

Making breadcrumbs

Save all the bits of left-over bread you cut off, like the crusts, and then toast them in a warm oven. You can pop them all into the oven after you have baked. They will toast as the oven cools down. When they are toasted, dried and crunchy, bash them with the end of a rolling pin in a bowl or blitz them in the food processor . They should be quite coarse crumbs when you are done. Once cool they will keep in an airtight container for ages. You can now make very many things with them, like scotch eggs, fish fingers or treacle tart. You can also make pasta taste fantastic if you melt some butter in a pan until very hot. Add a little salt and pepper and toss the crumbs in until crisp. Sprinkle over your pasta. If you sprinkle with sugar instead of salt and pepper and toast in hot brown butter they are fantastically nutty sprinkled on plain vanilla ice-cream.

Chapter Three

Research
Finding out which chicken lays which egg

Look at the pictures and see if you can guess who laid which egg.

Welsomers
Speckled hens that lay speckled eggs.

Silky Bantams
Perfect mothers and come in lots of colours. The eggs are small and of course lots of different colours.

Isa Brown
Isa Brown is a small and friendly hen and lays lots of paler brown eggs with bright yellow yolks. They love to live in groups and a single hen will lay up to 350 eggs in her life.

Morans
Morans are French and lay eggs like chocolate. They are beautiful birds who are great mums

Making a chicken out of an egg

Egg identification

Simply write in the name of the chicken from the page opposite, who you think laid the egg.
(Answers on the next page)

1. _____

2. _____

3. _____

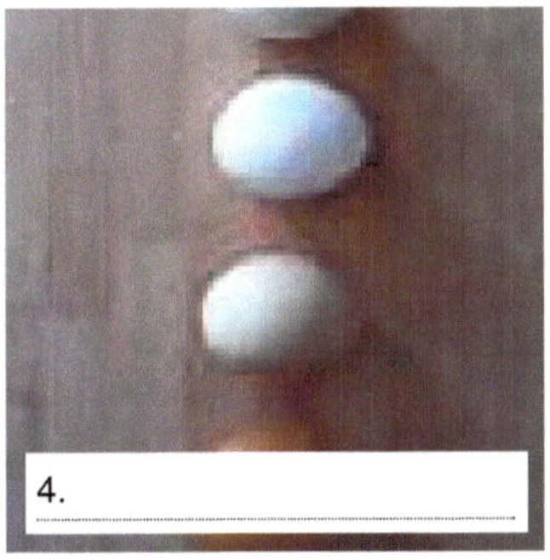

4. _____

5. _____

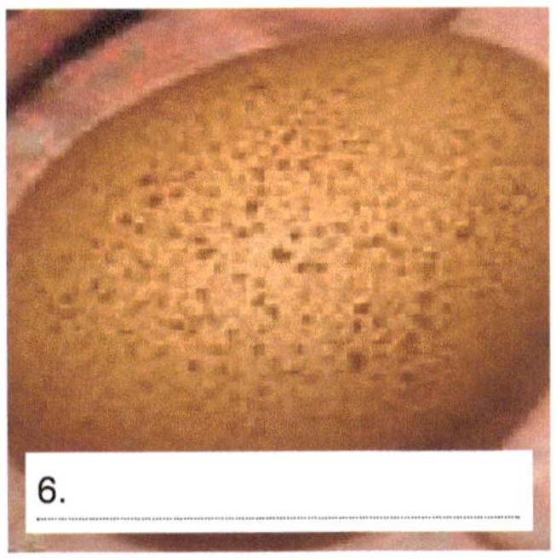

6. _____

7. _____

8. _____

9. _____

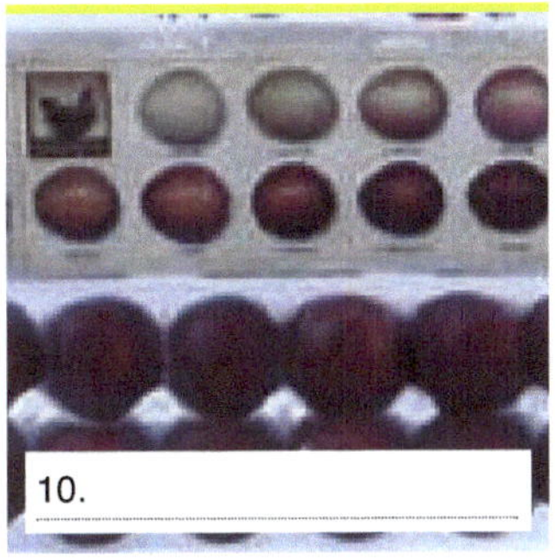

10. _____

51

Chapter Three

The egg shell

🥚

The wind took off with the sunset -
The fog came up with the tide,
When the Witch of the North took an Egg-shell
With a little Blue Devil inside.
"sink," she said, "or swim," she said,
"It's all you will get from me.
And that is the finish of him!" she said,
And the Egg-shell went to sea.
The wind fell dead with the midnight -
The fog shut down like a sheet,
When the Witch of the North heard the Egg-shell
Feeling by hand for a fleet.
"Get!" she said, "or you're gone," she said,
But the little Blue Devil said "No!"
The sights are just coming on," he said,
And he let the Whitehead go.
The wind got up with the morning -
The fog blew off with the rain,
When the Witch of the North saw the Egg-shell
And the little Blue Devil again.
"Did you swim?" she said. "did you sink?" she said,
And the little Blue Devil replied:
"For myself I swam, but I think," he said,
"There's somebody sinking outside."

Rudyard Kipling

Chapter Four

Eggs and broody hens

Chapter Four

Most people think that if an egg gets cold it will not hatch. This is not true. A hen will lay an egg each day until she has a good clutch to sit on. Ordinary chickens will go on laying an egg each day indefinitely, providing you keep stealing them. Some

chickens never go broody, whilst others can do it every month. If you leave eggs in the nest she will be stimulated to become broody by the sheer number of eggs. So size of clutch is the next cue to action if you are a chicken. Useful, this – it saves having to count the number of eggs or reason out the number of days you have been laying, which is way beyond the scope of any brainless hen.

This is very useful for the interested party who only wishes to hatch very special chicks, because you can replace the hens' eggs with any eggs you wish providing they are compatible and their bum and feet are the right size. For example a tiny Bantam will be a good mother for little French partridges.

If you find a broody, it is a good

idea to put her somewhere where she can sit quietly because she will stop all the other girls getting in the nest box and your egg production will drop. If you want her to stop being broody and start laying again you could put her somewhere draughty, like a cage with a wire bottom. They don't like the wind on their bums and will give up trying to sit eggs.

Looking after the eggs

It is important to store the eggs earmarked for hatching quite carefully. Egg boxes are perfect containers would you believe, or if you have a vast number of eggs you can use a sheet of corrugated tin. You need a rodent-proof shed (we don't want mouse tiddle all over the eggs) and ideally somewhere quite cold. It's a good idea not to clean the eggs off or douse them in water, because the shell is porous and wetting or rubbing the shell can push the bacteria into the egg. The eggs have a protective coating and washing and rubbing will destroy this. Just don't sit dirty eggs. All you need to do each day is turn the eggs over – in nature the hen would do this each time she laid a new egg, as it prevents the contents of the egg from sticking to the inside of the shell. If you are using the corrugated tin method you can simply take out the bottom egg and let the whole row gently roll down the tin. (Did I mention it has to be on a bit of a slope?)

You need to take a bit of care here or you will get hairline cracks in the shells, which is not conducive to effective hatching.

Eggs, more eggs and Labradors

This is the method used by some keepers when the pheasants in the laying pen start producing. Initially the eggs are not very fertile and not sent for hatching. This usually coincides with a massive glut of hens, ducks and geese eggs in the yard – it seems like eggs are coming out of the walls.

One year the Labrador really got into the swing of things. She made it her mission to find as many eggs as possible. This was Keeper's wife's fault. She had rewarded the first egg retrieved with a biscuit and so formed an association between eggs and food, and boy did this Lab like her food. Now, even though she was only allowed one biscuit a day, she worked all day to earn it.

She had several unpleasant experiences in her daily work because eggs are not always as innocent as they appear. She had been attacked by a ferocious Rhode Island as she attempted to steal her eggs, she had stung her nose and eyes badly in the nettle patch and been chased around the yard by a rampant gander. The worst thing that happened was when she found a nest of very old eggs. Keeper's wife took the first off her when she appeared at the back door with that silly grin that meant there was an egg in her mouth. It was in a terrible state and obviously about to explode at any minute. She took it gingerly outside and hurled it into the nettles. Sure enough it exploded as it landed, causing a flurry of disturbed hens and a stink that would perm your hair.

When the Lab arrived with a second very old egg, Keeper's wife refused to take it, turning the dog out of the house. She sat in the back yard, saliva dribbling out of the corners of her mouth but still gently cradling her booty. She was very persistent, but this time persistence did not pay off. Eventually the egg exploded, giving the dog the most unpleasant shock she ever had. She leapt into the air, gagging and shaking her head. She took off towards the pond, still spluttering and coughing. She drank long and hard from the pond, stopping from time to time to shake her head in disbelief. She gave up her summer egg-hunting job after that.

Making a hen broody

It's very easy to persuade your hens to stop messing about in the yard and go broody. If you stop collecting the eggs regularly you will find that they will all go off the lay and start brooding eggs instead. So all you have to do is leave something resembling a clutch of eggs in the nest box and they will be cued into action by the feel of a big clutch of eggs.

You used to be able to buy pot eggs but anything will do, I have even used golf balls when the golfer was preoccupied. Hens are really not bright enough to tell that you are cheating and will sit happily brooding golf balls for weeks if you don't replace them with real eggs. In fact you can keep them in this happy state in readiness for emergency foster care when eggs are deserted by the real mother for some reason.

Once you have substituted the golf balls with the real thing and she has warmed them to her body heat, the incubation period will start. This is why all the brood hatch at the same time – clever isn't it? Now it is absolutely vital that the eggs do not get cold.

It's jolly useful to have a permanently broody hen about the place if you are a keeper and often faced with little emergencies. For example, people out with their dogs off the lead often find what they think are abandoned eggs as the dog flushes the hen pheasant off her nest. Of course she will pretty soon abandon the eggs if this keeps happening, and pheasants do nest in some very daft places. Real bird brains, pheasants. The only good thing about them is the plumpness of their breasts as far as I am concerned.

Birds also get run over by cars or tractors during haymaking, leaving eggs or chicks to care for. For this reason hens often end up acting as foster carers to some very strange chicks. In fact being a keeper's hen pretty much guarantees that you will hatch anything other than chicken eggs.

Diagnosing broodiness

When you find a hen sitting in the nest box so tightly that she feels like she is superglued to the thing, when she gives a long, throaty warning cluck as you approach and attacks your hand like a screaming banshee, then the diagnosis might be 'broody'. To test out the diagnosis you need to slide your hand palm uppermost between her legs. It feels fantastic, soft and warm, almost makes you wish you were an embryo again, that is providing her pre-broody tension (PBT) hasn't triggered her to take your hand off. If she is broody she will attempt to round up your fingers by pedalling her feet and squeezing her wings. If you want a broody this is fantastic news. If you make your pocket money selling free range eggs it's a bit of a disaster, because you can pretty much guarantee that this hen is going to take a layer's holiday.

Choosing your broody

Like any good foster care the right match between young and carer must be considered. There are several things to think about. The first is length of time the eggs take to hatch; little bantams can hatch within 17 days whereas big breeds like Rhode Islands take up to 24 days. So, if you ask a bantam to hatch a clutch of duck eggs that need over 28 days she might get tired half way through and will be standing over a clutch of cold eggs when you go to feed her. Another danger is that she will not be spurred into the 'find food for babies' loop of her behavioural repertoire if the eggs hatch much too early, so you will end up with a brood of babies to rear yourself, not a happy prospect. The feeding part is manageable; it's the need to sit and brood every hour or so that is tedious and doing the housework with a brood of chicks inside your T-shirt is a little precarious.

Another thing to think about is the size and durability of the egg. It's no use putting dainty little bantam eggs under a hoofing great big, clumsy hen. She will crack the eggs as she tidies the nest and turns the eggs. Likewise it is asking a bit much of a little bantam to give her goose eggs, although I remember one valiant little girl sitting with one egg under each wing to finish off the hatching of some deserted eggs.

Caring for a broody

You will need to keep her in a safe place, as sitting hens are an easy meal for foxes. A box without a bottom is good because it allows the eggs to have contact with the moistness of the soil. There need to be holes in the box for airflow, but be sure they are not big enough to give rodents access to the hen – she won't like this and will probably dance about like a demented ferret and break all the eggs.

Leave her in a quiet place to do her job, lifting her once a day for

Eggs and broody hens

food, water and bowel relief. Stand well clear, as this is a lethal operation, ever heard the term 'foul smelling?' It could equally well be 'fowl smelling'. It's a good idea to encourage this operation well away from the broody box, as it is a magnet to foxes and small terriers, who love to roll in it.

When the eggs hatch she will need a safe place to rear her chicks and she will need feeding up. Hens often lose an awful lot of weight when they are broody. She will also need specialist food for the chicks. Ducks and geese do not thrive well on pheasant food. Feed this special food to the chicks behind a little slatted fence that the chicks can get through but the broody can't, that way she will not be gobbling up all your expensive chick food. Put pebbles or marbles in the water pot to stop the chicks falling in and getting soaked.

Chapter Four

Yum-Yum Corner
Custards Sweet or Savoury

Quick sweet custard

Mix together 2 tablespoons of sugar and one cup of powdered milk. Beat together one cup of fresh milk and 2 eggs and add to the sugar and powdered milk. Pour into a non-stick pan and place on a moderate heat. Stir continuously as the temperature rises and after about 4 minutes the mixture will begin to thicken. At this point remove from the heat and cool to room temperature to allow to set. Add vanilla extract for the traditional custard taste.

Now you have the custard you can impress folk with some pretty fancy puddings. You can use the custard for masses of different things. Simply add fruit, bananas, stewed apples or pears, or any type of berry (although these will stain the custard) or just pour it over your favourite pudding.

You can add loads of different things to make new puddings. Add cocoa to the powdered milk for chocolate sauce and serve in little bowls sprinkled with chocolate flakes. Add almond extract instead of vanilla or almond milk instead of plain milk and top with toasted almonds when set.

Add a double brandy or navy rum for an eggnog. If you leave out the vanilla you can use all manner of citrus flavours, but

you may need to increase the sugar if you are going for pure orange or lemon juice.

You can buy empty pastry cases and fill them with your custard and go wild with all sorts of fruit arrangements.

Use a large wine glass for a fancy effect. Even better if you own long spoons.

Floating islands

If you have masses of eggs to use up, you could make floating islands. Put a baking tray in the oven at 300°F with about an inch of water and allow to warm through without boiling. Just use one full egg and the yolks of two more to make the custard and allow to chill in a nice bowl. Whisk the remaining egg whites to stiff peaks and add 2 tablespoons of caster sugar and some vanilla, if that is the chosen flavour.

Take out the baking tray and use a big spoon to drop the mixture onto the surface of the water. Bake in the oven for about half an hour. Put the hot islands onto the cold custard and prepare to go to heaven!

Sweet custard and bread pudding

When the custard is smooth and warm, add 4 cups of diced stale bread and pour into a pudding dish. Sprinkle the top with nutmeg and bake in a hot oven for about 45 minutes or until a skewer comes out dry when you insert it into the middle of the pudding. Underdone is better than overdone. Serve with more custard or fruit.

You can jazz up this bread pudding in many different ways. Add dried fruit such as raisins or dates. Add chocolate, brown sugar or alcohol. Go citrus with oranges or lemons.

Sweet custard and bread and butter pudding

Remove the crusts from a stale sliced loaf. (You can make breadcrumbs out of these to coat fish etc.) Take half a pound of softened butter and grate the zest of a lemon onto it. Squeeze the juice of the lemon onto the butter and mix it all together. Butter the bread thickly with your lemon butter and cut across the diagonal.

Chapter Four

Gather together 2 tablespoons of sugar, some mixed spice, currants and nutmeg. Place a layer of bread into a greased pudding dish and sprinkle with currants and spice. Keep layering until no bread remains and end with the lemon butter on top. Pour in the custard. Now sprinkle the top with sugar and nutmeg. Bake in a moderate oven for 45 minutes or until the top is crispy brown. Serve with even more hot custard.

Again you can vary this basic bread and butter pudding with anything you fancy by replacing the currants and spice with other ingredients. Rhubarb and ginger is fantastic and very grown up.

Sweet custard and French toast

Cut the crusts off 6 slices of stale bread. Soak the bread in warm custard until it is soft. Melt some butter in a frying pan and fry off the bread on a warm heat until golden brown on both sides. Dust with icing sugar and top with apple sauce, pureed apricots or other fruit or berries.

Research
Finding out about custard tarts

Next time you go to the supermarket with the children, take a research note book with you. Take a good look at the custards.

Can you find both sweet custards and savoury custards?

Can you find both small and large custard tarts in the bakery section?

What are they called?

Can you find both small and large tarts in the grocery section?

What are they called?

Can you find empty tart cases to fill with your own custards?

Conclusions………………………………………………………………………
………………………………………………………………………………………
………………………………………………………………………………………

Cracking Eggs Experiment

In spring there may be a glut of eggs. It's a time for children to learn important things, like how to crack them without breaking the yolk.

If you can afford it, buy 12 of the smallest cheapest eggs in the store to experiment with at home. We are going to crack them into a bowl and separate the yolks from the whites using several different methods. You have to decide which you prefer.

Wash your hands and find two bowls, one for the yolks and one for the whites.

Method one

Hold the egg firmly in your preferred hand and hit it quite hard on the side of the bowl. If you have a hole in the egg put both your thumbs in the hole while still firmly holding the egg and pull your thumbs apart. Turn it over and the egg will fall out into the bowl. If you got this right first time give yourself a gold star. Keep trying until you get it, if it went wrong. It always goes wrong first time.

Method two

Now you can put your fingers under an egg yolk in your bowl and gently lift it out of the white. Pop it in the other bowl. Some people don't like the feel of the eggs, so they try to catch the yolk in one half of the shell as they pull the shell apart over the bowl with the whites in and then separate the yolk into the other bowl. Why not try this method and see which works best for you.

Method three

Some people don't like whacking the egg on the bowl and instead tap gently at the shell with the blade of a knife. When the hole is big enough pull the shell apart in the same way. Other people smack the egg hard on the table top and pull apart.

You can buy a little piece of

Chapter Four

equipment that will do the job for you. It is like a dish with a hole in that the white can escape through but the yolk cannot.

Whichever method you choose there are two things you must never, never do. The first is to get bits of eggshell in the egg. The second is to break the yolk. If you get yolk in with the whites, it will not let your whites whisk into frothy peaks so you won't be able to make soufflés and meringues.

Use the eggs you break to make an omelette or floating meringues if your whites will whisk. If you have perfect yolks you could try making mayonnaise or marzipan. You will find recipes for both of these on line.

Custard pie fights

Custard pie fights came about in the early days of black and white films. Usually today people throw paper plates with foam rather than custard. I don't really approve of play fights with food, but I must confess to being

involved in a few in days gone by. Custard is OK for a fight, as it doesn't injure the victim and doesn't smell as bad as rotten eggs.

The dinner table was always a danger point when the family was sitting waiting for the next thing to happen. The messiest fight was started one Sunday lunchtime by the baby. She innocently whacked a spoonful of custard at Keeper as his wife entered with a huge bowl of strawberry jelly. The children were rolling with laughter as Keeper wiped custard from his forehead. Keeper, who always went too far, loaded his dessert spoon and took aim at each child individually and then let rip at eldest son. The poor chap was always first to be picked on.

The boy reacted badly, clawing at the muck on his face and saying words not strictly permitted at the dinner table. Seeing the boy didn't like a face full of custard, the girls decided to join in. Before long the bowl of custard was almost gone amid screams of delight from all, so they started throwing the red jelly. The dining end of the living room was now awash with jelly and custard and the laughter had reached the stage where everyone's face was beginning to ache. Keeper's wife threw a huge wodge of paper napkins into the mess on the table, thinking it might focus their minds on surrender and cleaning up. No such luck. Eldest son made a square receptacle out of a napkin, filled it with gravy from the left-behind gravy boat and began the second round of the food fight. Soon they were all making bombs out of napkins and gravy. Keeper's wife's eyes fell on the huge jug of water in the middle of the table. She snatched it up and headed for the kitchen before it became ammunition for round three in the shape of water bombs.

By now the baby was animated, little arms and legs thrashing about shrieking with delight. The others were now all in a terrible state. Bits of tissue, gravy, jelly and custard were stinging their faces and eyes. 'Mum, it's up my nose and everything smells of gravy. Help me!'

Focus on the clean-up, kids. It'll keep your mind off the discomfort whilst we wait for the Rayburn to heat up enough water to bath you all.

Chapter Five

Chickens as foster mothers

Chickens as foster mothers

All the hens in the gamekeeper's yard are destined to become foster mothers. If they don't oblige or get it wrong, they end up in the pot. So the only reason gamekeepers keep hens is to provide foster mothers for a variety of different game birds. These broody hens arrive from lots of different places, but usually from a neighbour who has a broody and is glad to lend her to hatch a brood of pheasants. Save feeding her while she is off the lay. Most of these broodies were housed on the rearing field with their clutches of eggs and pheasant chicks. Keeper's wife got involved when clutches of partridges arrived, usually due to some mishap, and needed a very small broody.

Learning about partridges

There are two different types of partridge in Britain, Grey and French. The ones you see are probably French, because the little Grey is very rare now.

Grey partridges

Grey partridges arrived in Great Britain after the Ice Age. Records from a century ago show that they were the most popular game bird for shooting. Country gentlemen and their friends shot more than 2 million each year between 1870 and 1930. It was the gamekeeper's job to put as many over the guns as he could. They did this by hand-rearing eggs and chicks under broody hens, taking very good care of all wild stock and shooting predators. Major predators were foxes and birds of prey.

The grey partridge has almost disappeared from the countryside today. They are quite a drab little bird and live off seeds and insects. When farmers started spraying fields with insecticides to stop insects eating their crops the little bird lost a major part of its food supply. Farmers also ripped out the hedgerows so that they could use bigger farm vehicles like tractors and combine harvesters, and this destroyed the habitat favoured by grey partridges.

French partridges

French partridges are also called red-legged partridges and are bigger than grey partridges. They are very beautiful. The male has a very distinct call. He goes 'chuck-chukka-chuff' when he calls his mate or babies. They form pair bonds and both the male and female rear the babies. It has been noted that sometimes the female will build two nests and lay eggs in both. They then put all the eggs together as they hatch and rear them as one big family. This is called a covey. They are very protective of their young and will fake injury to tease a predator away from the nest and young. You may have seen them in a country lane running along, dragging their wing along the ground pretending to be an easy catch. Once they have led you away from their young they will fly off and rejoin them. They stay together in a family until the following mating season.

As the French partridge has increased, the little grey partridge is seen less and less. That doesn't necessarily mean the French partridge is somehow responsible for the decline, but they do eat the same food, so competition for diet may be a major factor. When partridge chicks hatch they are able to feed themselves and follow the parents, but they can't maintain their own body weight and temperature (thermo-regulation) without eating a huge amount of insects in the first two weeks of life. Another thing that affects this is rainfall. So when we have lots of rain just at the time when these tiny babies, about the size of a bumble bee, are hatching they can get so cold they just die.

Back to the yard: being a foster mother to partridges

May is a dangerous time for the ground nesting partridge, coinciding as it does with hay making. Partridges are extremely persistent in guarding their nests and will sometimes sit so tight that they are run over by the tractor. Other times their nest is missed and the eggs survive, but the nest is left so exposed as to render the hatching impossible. When this happens caring humans will sometimes keep the eggs warm inside their shirts and deliver them to the keeper. This is just what happened one glorious day in May. A sweet little bantam had just gone broody and was given the still-warm eggs. Bantams only take 17 days to hatch so it wouldn't matter too much that the partridge eggs were part way through their incubation.

One day in June the little brood hatched, perfectly sweet little things looking just like bumble bees. They were kept warm and well fed by the little bantam and grew at a remarkable pace, she of course having no idea that they were not chickens.

One day in August when the sun was shining and the wind didn't blow, the mother bantam went for a walk around the yard with her little brood of chicks. They were six weeks old now and not too big for their age. They had appeared a little strange to her ever since they hatched. In fact they still looked more like bees than chickens.

French and grey partridge chicks

Even though they were unusual chicks, the bantam was not prepared for the next thing that happened on this beautiful sunny day. As she crossed the yard all the chicks suddenly took off and flew into the

Chapter Five

air. They landed in a row on the roof of the barn.

Can you imagine the look of sheer disbelief on the hen's face, beak open, head on one side, clearly thinking 'Wow! How did they do that?' She was dimly aware that chickens don't fly like that. The best a chicken can do is to clumsily flap up into a tree at night so that the foxes cannot eat her. Of course she had no idea that her eggs had been replaced with partridge eggs. All she knew was that she had hatched a very unusual brood of chicks. This was clearly not her fault, since she had been a textbook mother. She had kept the eggs warm until they hatched, turning them over every day so that the babies did not stick to the inside of the eggshell. Eventually they all hatched. She then showed the tiny chicks how to eat insects. She snuggled them under her wings to keep warm when they were cold or when it was dark or raining. Now the ungrateful brood had taken off and flown as if they were wild birds, not chickens. She stood in the yard and watched in amazement. Then she wondered, as mothers often do, just where she had done wrong.

Fostering to ducklings

One rainy day at the end of an April that had more than its share of April showers, a big, fat, brown hen named Elsie was taking her new brood out for their first walk around the yard in search of food. The brood was black and yellow and very fluffy. There were twelve altogether. They had taken 28 days to hatch, much longer than usual

to hatch, so the broody hen was cock-a-hoop to be free of the broody box.

Her eggs had been laid on the side of the lake by a Mallard Duck. A couple out walking their dog found the eggs and thought they had been deserted. What probably happened was their dog scared Mum off the nest and she slid into the water to escape it's attentions. If they had left the eggs alone she would have returned to

Chickens as foster mothers

them as soon as they were out of sight. By the time the eggs arrived at Keeper's cottage they were already chilling so they were tucked up under Elsie who had been broody for a couple of days.

Now instead of swimming along behind their mother they were blessed with a mother who justifiably thought they were chickens.

Elsie talked to the youngsters as she slowly walked around the yard. cwork, cwork. She pecked pointedly at likely sources of food and scratched at the straw and earth in the yard to flush out any insect life or grains left over from the morning feeding frenzy. The chicks replied with peep, peep as they ran to keep up and jostled for position. After a while the hen stopped and spread her wings to allow the babies to rest and shelter against her warm breast. She seemed a little surprised when half of them climbed onto her back rather than creeping underneath her to get warm. Nevertheless, this was a seriously blissful mother.

This bliss was soon to turn to blind panic as she stood up to continue the search for food and happened to pass the pond where the ducks were swimming around with their newly hatched broods. As soon as her brood saw the water they made a dash for it. She squawked and squealed a warning at them as loudly as she could. She danced about, leaping from one leg to another, running up and down the edge of the pond. She was too afraid to go in after them for she knew for sure that no ordinary chicks and chickens could swim. As her young plopped into the water and bobbed about like pieces of cotton wool she realised that she had hatched a very special clutch of eggs.

She paced the edge of the huge pond calling to the brood every so often. They blissfully ignored her as they bobbed about in a tight knit group. Eventually they were approached by a huge duck who swam round and round them seeming to wonder where these tiny babies had come from. This set the ducklings into a panic and they finally heeded the cries of the old, brown broody and headed for the bank. They snuggled their little wet bodies under the hen right there on the edge of the pond. She seemed to know instinctively that many a duckling has died of the wet because even though they spend a good deal of time in the water their down is not watertight like the feathers of an adult.

After that the old brown hen waited patiently each day for the chicks to finish their swim and allowed them to snuggle under her to get dry when they had finished their essential water practice. She seemed very proud of her unusual chicks and soon accepted the daily routine using the time when the ducklings were swimming to scratch about on the edge of the pond for tasty morsels like baby frogs. What she didn't know of course was that they were Mallard ducklings and that she, Elsie, had turned out to be really great a foster mother.

A novel way of fostering

Now here is a very strange predator-prey relationship. These kitties are taking advantage of an obliging old hen to keep warm whilst their Mum was off hunting for mice. Purrfectly safe. I wonder if the chicken will be safe when that little brood grow up.

Not so sure about the next situation either. Don't think I would trust a cat with baby chickens. I've seen them play with mice. They play rough.

What a motley crew

By the end of the rearing season it was not uncommon to have three or

four broodies sitting on motley collections of eggs from different kinds of birds. Whilst trying to keep broodies with the same species to hatch if possible, time to hatching was most important when deciding who to give stray eggs to for emergency care. People turned up with a huge variety of casualties as the summer

wore on and guesses had to be made about the species and how far the eggs were through their incubation period. When the hen feels the movement of hatching chicks she is cued to the next stage and will abandon any unhatched eggs to care for the chicks. It is vital then to do a daily check to see who has hatching eggs and to make sure the ones about to hatch are all under the same hen. Two big problems with this method are that a hen can end up with a motley crew of ducklings, pheasants, partridges and a bantam or she can end up as a sort of career broody, being kept sitting in waiting for the whole summer. Of course it is always the most obliging hen that gets the longest and most tedious sit.

A professional carer

Such a situation arose for one dedicated professional carer, a big, brown Rhode Island, a breed not known for its prowess as broodies. Wendy was an exception to the rule, and she had done more than her share of warming up and keeping warm. She had got to the point of hatching very many eggs only to have them finished off by a hen with a larger brood whilst she proffered emergency care to pheasant eggs found on the side of the road. These were about to hatch when a clutch of French partridge eggs needed finishing off. As she was such a good broody she lost her pheasant eggs to another and had to start again with the partridges. She lost these after two weeks of incubation to a broody with smaller feet and ended up with one strange-

Chapter Five

shaped egg. This she was allowed to hatch. And so it was that she spent the entire summer brooding eggs only to end up with… a PEACOCK!

Would you guess that a chick that ugly would grow into something that beautiful?

Yum-Yum Corner
Savoury Custard

You make this custard in the normal way, but leave out the sugar and add herbs and seasoning. You can also replace the milk with tomato juice.

Savoury custard and French toast

Cut the crusts off 6 slices of stale bread. Soak the bread in warm savoury custard until it is soft. Melt some butter in a frying pan and fry off the bread on a warm heat until golden brown on both sides. Cover with your favourite breakfast ingredients like bacon, mushrooms, tomatoes or black pudding.

Baking custard in the oven

You can make custards in the oven as well as on top of the stove. The texture is very different and can be used for both hot and cold dishes.

Begin by heating the oven to between 180 and 200 degrees, depending on your oven. Now choose a deep baking dish that holds about a pint. We are going to make a plain custard that you can serve to poorly people who need to be spoiled.

Method one

Butter the sides of the baking dish. Warm through ¾ pint of milk. Beat 2 eggs in a bowl with 1 ounce of sugar and a few drops of vanilla. Just before the milk boils pour it over the eggs whisking as you pour. Now pour it into the baking dish and sprinkle nutmeg on the top. Pop in the oven for 50–60 minutes. It is done when it just wobbles and the tip of a knife comes out clean when you stick it in.

Chapter Five

Method two

Butter the dish as before. This time whisk 4 eggs in a bowl and add 1 pint of cold milk, 1 ounce of sugar and some vanilla. Mix really well and then pour through a strainer to catch possible little bits of fatty egg. Pour into the baking dish and cook for 60 to 80 mins. This may take a little longer as you are starting with cold ingredients.

Both of these methods work well poured into a pastry case before cooking and both are best eaten cold.

Blind pastry cases for custard tarts and quiches

Shortcrust pastry will do for both of these. You can buy pastry ready made from the supermarket. This is so good it's hardly worth making your own. You can use the same shortcrust pastry for both savoury and sweet tarts. You can make different sizes by using a range of tins. A sponge cake tin is good for big one, Yorkshire pudding tins for four small ones or little cake tins for a quiche that you can eat in one bite. Best not use muffin tins because they are so deep the egg doesn't cook through before the pastry is overcooked.

Line a well-greased tin with pastry. Prick the bottom to stop it rising. Cover with greaseproof paper and pour in something to hold the paper down whilst the pastry cooks. This is really important if you have a fan oven because the fan blows the paper away. I have a jar of old, dried butter beans that I have used so often they are now baked hard like bullets. This is called 'blind baking' a pastry case. They need to cook for 15 minutes or so at 160 in my oven but yours might be different. Less time of course for very small cases. You need to experiment. It's good to get to know how to do this as you can make loads of different recipes with them. Keep some in the freezer for when people surprise you with a visit.

Savoury tarts

Make a blind baking case, or several at one time as they keep really well. Flavour your baked custard mix with masses of your favourite herbs and seasonings, pour into the pastry case and bake in a moderate oven for about 40 minutes.

Savoury egg tart

While the pastry is cooking you can prepare the fillings. Crack 4 eggs into a bowl and whisk well with ¾ pint of milk. Pour the baked custard mix into the pastry case and then crack 4 fresh eggs into the custard and bake.

Savoury custard and bacon and egg pie

Fry chopped bacon until crispy and line the bottom of the pastry base. Pour on the baked custard mix flavoured with herbs and seasoning, sprinkle with parsley and bake.

Now you have got going you will think of dozens of ways to use baked custard mix. My own favourite if cheese and spinach. Any leftover meats are good. Almost all vegetables, even potatoes will go in and the custard will take almost any type of cheese both in it and sprinkled on top.

Chapter Five

Research
Savoury Custards and Quiche

Next time you go to the supermarket with the children, take a research note book with you. Take a good look at the savoury tarts and quiches.

How many different flavours of savoury tart can you see?

How many different flavours can you find?

Which one would you like to eat?

Did you find tarts in lots of different places in the store?

Sweet egg custards and savoury tarts are quite different. Write down three things you have noted that make them different.

Designer eggs for tea

In this experiment we are going to personalise your teatime eggs. You will need eggs, birthday candles and food colouring.

Begin by making sure the raw eggs are very clean and dry. Now use the birthday candle to draw any design you want on an egg. Try to cover the entire egg. The wax from the candle might be nearly invisible, but don't worry the design will show through when the egg is coloured. When all the eggs are covered in artwork, boil a pan of water and add your food colouring. Pop in the eggs and boil for your favourite time. If you are going to give them as presents it is best to hard boil them.

At the end of the time lift out your eggs and you should have a coloured, personally designed egg.

Chickens as foster mothers

Five Little Ducks

Five little ducks went swimming one day,
Over the hill and far away,
Mother duck said "Quack, quack, quack,"
And only four little ducks came back.

Four little ducks went swimming one day,
Over the hill and far away,
Mother duck said "Quack, quack, quack,"
And only three little ducks came back.

Three little ducks went swimming one day,
Over the hill and far away,
Mother duck said "Quack, quack, quack,"
And only two little ducks came back.

Two little ducks went swimming one day,
Over the hill and far away,
Mother duck said "Quack, quack, quack,"
And only one little duck came back.

One little duck went swimming one day,
Over the hill and far away,
Mother duck said "Quack, quack, quack,"
And all those five little ducks came back!

Chapter Six

Sexing Chickens

Sexing Chickens

Pair of chickens   Pair of turkeys   Pair of pheasants

Chicken sexers can tell the difference between male and female chicks as soon as they hatch. They earn a lot of money because they save the poultry farmer a lot of money. It is however very difficult to do, because male and female chicks look so very alike. You also need to have lots of practice to become a good chicken sexer.

When they are older, it is easy to tell which is the male and which the female. The feathers are different, the wattle and combs are different and the female is almost always smaller than the male. Wattles are the red dangly bits under the throat and combs are the red bits on top of the head. These are usually redder and bigger in males. Another random fact is that when a chicken is not well these red things will become pale, just like a poorly child.

Now it's very difficult. In fact the only thing you can be sure of is that they will either be boys or girls, that is cocks or hens. A 50/50 chance.

What about these little darlings?

As they get their feathers and wattles and combs it becomes easier for the amateur like you and me to sex them.

Chapter Six

If you have a good-sized brood to compare with each other it is easier still. Even so it is often a guess, and sometimes not noticeable until the point of lay.

All this is not so important in the yard, where you are happy to eat the cockerels if you have too many and gamekeepers certainly don't mind the sex of the birds. But if you are hatching birds commercially It is really important to be able to tell males from females, because eventually the males will be a lot bigger than the females. Imagine you had hatched 1000 turkey eggs in June. If you fed them all until Christmas the food bill would be astronomical. At Christmas the females would be 10–12 pounds, which is the favourite weight. The males (stags) on the other hand would be enormous at 20–30 pounds. These are almost impossible to sell. So male turkeys are not kept until a few weeks before Christmas, because most hatcheries want hens. It is the same perhaps for little people like you and me. We don't want a yard full of squabbling cockerels come the autumn.

So now we know that when poultry hatch it is very difficult to tell if they are male or female. Sometimes you cannot tell until they start to lay eggs or are at the point of lay. When a chicken is about to start laying eggs, she is called a pullet. This is the best time to buy chickens if you want to keep them in your garden or yard.

That's not a pullet, it's a cockerel

One day in January the gamekeeper's wife went to market, where she found the cutest little pullets for sale. They were black with little red spots and were called Partridge Wyndotts. She bought six and took them home, where she put them in a stable to keep warm and safe. Next day she began to feed them on layers' mash. This is very special food that makes hens lay eggs. After a few days the gamekeeper's wife found one beautiful little brown egg in the nest box when she fed the hens. It was a rather strange egg. It had a soft shell. She didn't quite know what to do with a soft-shelled egg.

Sexing Chickens

The next day she found another egg. The shell was hard this time, but the egg had a point at each end. How would she know which end to put in the eggcup?

The next day there was another unusual egg. It was enormous. When the gamekeeper's wife used the egg to make a custard tart, she found it had two yolks inside. Soon she was collecting five little eggs every day, and every so often one would be a very strange egg indeed.

The keeper's wife wondered why there were only five eggs when she had bought six pullets. She couldn't tell which hen was being lazy, so she didn't know what to do, although she could tell which one was a bossy boots.

One day she noticed that Bossy Boots had a funny little red lump on her head. Day by day the lump got bigger and bigger. It stuck right up on Bossy Boots' head like a big red comb stuck in its feathers.

The gamekeeper's wife had guessed what was happening now, but the bird still behaved like all the others except for being bossy. One day, very early in the morning, Bossy Boots had an urge to fly up onto the roof. Here she stood puffing out her chest and thrusting her head up and down. Suddenly, as the bird stretched its neck high into the air, a horrible noise came from her beak - cock a doodle doo!

Aha! One of the pullets was a cockerel. So another difference between male and female chickens is that the males crow. I never heard of a hen that crowed. There is an old saying that 'a whistling woman and a crowing hen is neither fit for god nor men.' I don't really know what this means, but it shows that both are rather rare.

Chapter Six

Yum-Yum Corner
Using up strange shaped eggs and blind cases

Custard Tart

For a custard tart you do not need to make custard – it happens in the oven. Start with 6 eggs beaten with a pint of milk. For an egg custard add 2 tablespoons of sugar and pour the mixture into your pastry case. It's a good idea to stand your pastry case in a tray and put it inside the oven to pour in the mixture, then it doesn't get spilt everywhere. Now you can sprinkle nutmeg on the top if you like it. Cook at 160 for about 20 to 30 minutes or until the mixture is just wobbly.

Quiche (savoury custard tart)

For the quiche chop up an onion really small and do the same with 4 slices of bacon. Gently fry these until golden brown. Add pepper but not much salt, because the bacon will make it salty. Place these in your blind pastry case and pour over the custard mix after you have grated some cheddar cheese in.

Cook at 160° for about 20 minutes or until the mixture is just wobbly. You can use all different things in the quiche. I like broccoli and cheese with walnuts. Anything you like really but not tomatoes because these make everything wet and soggy. Chipolatas are good or fish like tuna and smoked mackerel.

Savoury tarts

Make a blind baking case, or several at one time as they keep really well. Flavour your custard with masses of your favorite herbs and seasonings, pour into the pastry case and bake in a moderate oven for about 40 minutes.

Savoury egg tart

Pour the savoury custard into the pastry case and then crack 4 fresh eggs whole into the whisked egg and milk custard and bake.

Savoury custard and bacon and egg pie

Fry chopped bacon until crispy and line the bottom of the pastry case. Pour on the savoury custard flavoured with herbs and seasoning, sprinkle with parsley and bake.

Savoury custard and sausage tart

Cook the sausages first or use leftover ones if they are not too well cooked. Put them in the bottom of a blind case and cover with your savoury custard mix.

Now you have got going you will think of dozens of ways to use savoury custard. My own favorite is cheese and spinach. Any leftover meats are good. Almost all vegetables, even potatoes will go in and the custard will take almost any type of cheese both in it and sprinkled on

Chapter Six

top. Tomatoes and courgettes can make the whole thing soggy. Two things to remember are that the meat and vegetables you put in need to be precooked if they are not going to be too underdone but not too well cooked if they are not to be overcooked. More experiments here. Secondly, you will need less custard mix because of the space your fillings take up. It's a good idea to put the tins with the custard in inside a bigger baking tray is case he custard boils over.

Research
Find out about shop bought pastry

Next time you take the children to the supermarket, take your notebook with you. Take a good look at the ready-made pastry. How many different kinds of pastry do they have? What are they called? What is the difference between block and ready rolled pastry?

Try to decide which pastry would be best for the following things:

1. Sausage rolls
2. Mince pies
3. Jam puffs
4. Apple pies
5. Cheese straws

Conclusions……………………………………………………………………………
…………………………………………………………………………………………
…………………………………………………………………………………………
…………………………………………………………………………………………
…………………………………………………………………………………………
…………………………………………………………………………………………

Experiments with pastry

Give your children the left-over pastry and let them experiment with little tarts and pies, both sweet and savoury. One of mine likes to make savoury biscuits. He rolls out the pastry into a square. Then he grates on some cheese and experiments with dried herbs sprinkled over the top. He then rolls the pastry up tight into a long sausage and cuts up into little thin rounds. He places them all on a baking tray and sprinkles with sea salt, then bakes for about 10 minutes until crisp. Delicious with cheese.

You can do the same with sweet biscuits. Roll the pastry into a square again but this time sprinkle with sugar and spices like cinnamon, nutmeg, cardamom or cloves. Now sprinkle currants over the pastry and squash them into the pastry with a rolling pin. Now roll in up tight as before and cut into thin rounds. Bake for 10 minutes until crisp. You now have perfect squashed fly biscuits. You can use lots of different things to flavour your biscuits. Chocolate chips or candied peel are good, just steer clear of anything moist like strawberries or raspberries because these will make you mix wet and you will get soggy biscuits. Smarties didn't work well when littlest son tried them.

Chapter Six

Cock a doodle do!

Cock a doodle do!
My dame has lost her shoe,
My master's lost his fiddlestick,
And knows not what to do.
Cock a doodle do!
What is my dame to do?
Till master's found his fiddlingstick,
She'll dance without her shoe.

Cock a doodle do!
My dame has found her shoe,
And master's found his fiddlingstick,
Sing cock a doodle do!

Chapter Seven

Battery Hens and Eggs

Chapter Six

Where do the eggs you eat come from? If you buy cheap supermarket eggs you can pretty much guess that the life the chicken led was gruesome. Battery hens are kept in cages that do not allow them to spread their wings. Each cage is narrower than one bird stretched out. Typically, three birds are kept in a cage. They have an area the size of a leaflet to stand on for their entire life. Their beaks are removed so that they cannot kill each other with their pecking. Even so they usually suffer loss of feathers due to the cramped conditions. They are kept in artificial light to keep them laying. The eggs roll out of the cage when laid, unless the dead body of another hen gets in the way. Life for the hen is short, brutish and cruel, just like nature you might say. Usually, the only escape for the hen is the slaughterhouse.

If you want to know more about the life of a battery hen, just go to your favourite search engine and type in battery hens. You may even find an opportunity to join the Save Hens Campaign.

Most of the eggs we buy in the supermarket are laid by hens which are kept in tiny cages in very large, noisy, smelly, cramped buildings. They live together in very crowded cages and have their beaks removed to stop them pecking each other. They still manage to pull out each other's feathers though. Debeaking stops them actually eating each other. This way of keeping hens is called a battery. The eggs are all infertile. This means they do not have a baby chick in them because these hens never meet a cockerel, their world in entirely female. So…

Hens can lay eggs without being mated.

Hens do not have to be happy to lay eggs.

Battery hens are not battery operated.

Battery hens never see daylight. They lay more eggs if they think it is light outside so the farmers fool them with electric lights, and they even lay lots of eggs in the winter when it gets dark early. So you can adjust a hen's day with artificial light and fool them into laying more than once a day, which is what nature intended.

Battery hens are fed on the cheapest possible rubbish food. This is fed to them automatically. They do not need to scratch and peck to find food. Consequently life is very, very boring. Because the food provided is the cheapest possible, battery hens lay the cheapest possible eggs – rubbish eggs.

A battery hen begins to lay eggs at an early age and when she stops laying she is killed. This usually all takes less than a year. If you rescue a battery hen at the end of her sentence and treat her very kindly, she will start laying eggs for your tea. Farmers are often happy to give them away rather than kill them at this time because the body of a battery hen is not worth anything. They don't make good eating. They will live for several more years if you rescue them and will make you laugh as they begin to live in the real world.

Making a new hen out of an old battery

One day in December when it was cold and grey, six scruffy hens arrived in the yard. They had come from a chicken farm where they had laid about 250 eggs in as many days and were all laid out. They looked an absolute sight. Their beaks were missing, so they had to turn their heads upside down to eat, the feathers stuck out on their wings and their breasts and bottoms were practically bald. They almost looked oven ready.

Until now they had lived in very small cages with enough to eat and drink but very little space. They fought with each other and plucked each other's feathers if they could get a grip with their cut off beaks. They had probably produced an egg or more every day but never got to see it because it rolled away as soon as it was laid. Hens that went broody in this environment were taken away and never seen again, so there were never any chicks about. As you know, hens reared like this are called battery hens. These hens are even more stupid than regular hens in the yard.

For these poor old things the real world must have looked very large. The bald hens cuddled together. They were very cold and very miserable. Keeper's wife felt sorry for the poor old things and shushed them into a stable that she filled with nice warm

Chapter Six

straw. She made them nourishing, warm chicken mash and gave them fresh water. She shut the door tightly to keep out the cold and went to bed. After a day or two the hens stopped huddling together and began to walk around the stable. They still didn't separate but went everywhere together. If one hen went for a drink, all six hens went for a drink. If one hen tried out a new perch, all six hens tried out a new perch.

The food they were given was delicious and as their beaks grew back they soon found they could catch other sources of food, like spiders and bugs.

One day, to her surprise, one of the hens laid an egg. She had never seen anything so beautiful before. It was ovoid perfection. The others gathered around and just stared. When Keeper's wife came to feed the hens she was delighted to see the egg. She brought in some nesting boxes and filled them with lovely soft hay. Soon all six hens were laying an egg every day and spring was here.

Come spring and the bottom of the stable door was left open in the day so that the hens could go for a walk. They were now fully feathered and looked like proper hens of no specific breed. At first they reluctantly explored the area in front of the stable. They were fearful. They knew nothing. They ran from other birds in the yard, screeched at the gander, were startled at a pheasant calling up his females, 'Cock up, cock up'. Everything for them was new and scary and different. It was as if they didn't know the language everyone else was squawking or clucking.

Now the stable door was left open in the day, the hens could go for a walk. They tried out many new things and gave much entertainment to the watcher. If one hen tried climbing a log, flapping and fussing and making a terrible din, pretty soon all six were at it. If one flew up a tree, they all tried flying up a tree. If one tried pulling a worm out of the ground whilst Keeper dug the vegetable patch and ate it, the others also tried worms for lunch. One of their favourite things to do was to follow Keeper's wife as she mowed the lawn, pecking at the insect life that was displaced by the mowing. Their motto seemed to be 'everything in unison'.

Battery Hens and Eggs

They slowly began trying out many new things. Still in unison, they explored and tried climbing a log. One began scratching in the yard for food, and everyone stated scratching and pecking. One hen flew up a yew tree and they all joined her. Finding a rotting rat body, they all leapt squawking on the heap of maggots it had produced. Yum Yum! The noise they made attracted other birds in the yard. Soon they were surrounded by poultry and game and their feast was stolen from under their beaks.

Slowly they began to behave like normal hens, but remained very attached to each other. They were also always a little strange. Visitors would ask 'what's wrong with those weird hens?' The other birds knew they were weird too.

Now confusion reigned as they were chivvied about by local residents. They lost each other and panic set in. Most of the birds in the yard ignored them and kept their distance from these very different newcomers. They didn't much like the neurotic behaviour our birds displayed as they ran around, necks stretched out, squawking fit to die. Others in the yard, the bullies who would fall out with anything that was too small or the wrong colour to fit in, set about any of our hens within pecking distance. Pretty soon our birds found their way back into the safety of the stable and buried themselves in hay. The strange thing was that the local residents left them to it. No other bird went into the stable. Weird, eh?

Eventually the strangers began to fit in and became part of the yard gang. Later in the year one or two of them submitted to the romance of the cockerel and hatched a few chicks of their own. They often got their timing wrong though, as you will discover when you read the story of the Christmas cockerel.

At first just one of the hens went broody and sat on her eggs to hatch them. Before all the rest could follow her lead, Keeper's wife took her away to a nice safe broody box and sat her on pot eggs. She could not hatch her own eggs because she had never met a cockerel, so her eggs were infertile. By now the pheasants were beginning to lay the very early eggs. These were often not very fertile and Keeper's

Chapter Six

wife used them to make cakes and custards for tea. She gathered twelve nice-looking pheasant eggs, making sure there were no hairline cracks in them and that they were a regular size, and put them under the old hen. She was not sure whether the old battery hen would damage the eggs, for they were smaller than the eggs the hen laid, or if she would make a good mother. Since the eggs were early eggs and she was only going to use them for baking, she decided to take a chance.

After 24 days there was a scratching and a peeping coming from the eggs when the old hen was lifted for food. Next day she had seven beautiful, striped chicks and one black one. She made a wonderful foster mother and reared all seven of the chicks. She showed them all the new tricks she had learned when she had come from the chicken farm, how to eat insects and worms, how to perch on logs and most important how to roost in trees so that they were not eaten at night by predators. They grew up to be perfect pheasants. The hen never suspected that they were not her own, not even when they flew off into the woods, soaring high above the trees practising their flight for that fatal day in November when the guns would be out.

It just goes to show it's never too late to try the good life.

The Christmas cockerel

One Christmas morning, Keeper's wife went out to feed corn to the hens. She called 'come, come, come, come!' Chickens came from everywhere as the feeding frenzy began. They flew down from trees, crashed out of bushes, popped out from under Land Rovers and wheelbarrows and tripped over the stable doors. They never, never appeared out of the undergrowth at the edge of the thicket, because if they were daft enough to roost out there they were usually fox food by morning.

Today however one very small bantam appeared from a clump of dead nettles. She was making that familiar strange 'caw, caw' sound. I'm sure you know now what that means. She ran up and gobbled down food as if she was starving. Then, to the

Keeper's wife's surprise, one fluffy, mottled chick ran out of the dead nettles and joined his bantam mum.

The corn was far too big for him to eat. He would surely die as the weather was so cold and he was not very safe in the patch of nettles. Heaven knows how the bantam had survived the foxes sitting in the undergrowth, and how on earth she had hatched a chick at the coldest time of the year in a such a dangerous place is a mystery.

It took the whole family to catch the bantam and her chick, Little Son eventually cornering the two behind the log heap. Soon they were locked up safe in the stable where the chick was given boiled eggs for tea until some proper food could be purchased. To everyone's surprise he did not die. In fact he grew into the smartest, toughest, loudest cockerel we ever owned. The following summer there were lots of chickens hatched who grew up to look just like him.

Chicken is the best Sunday roast and so easy to do, if not quite as easy as

Chapter Six

Yum-Yum Corner
Chicken roast: the basic method

boiling an egg. The chicken we buy in the supermarket has been prepared for cooking. It has been plucked and drawn. Drawn means taking out the insides, not making a picture. Usually the legs are tied together with elastic and the bird is trussed up. This is called 'oven ready'. Sometimes you can buy chickens 'long legged'. This means they have been plucked but have not had their insides taken out or their legs removed.

If the bird you bought has the neck, heart and gizzard inside in a bag, you can use these to make fantastic gravy. Usually these giblets are missing these days.

Before you start your Sunday lunch you need to be sure that everything is very clean and wash your hands every time you handle the bird. Chicken can have germs, and there is one, called e-coli, that can make you and your family very ill. These germs are all killed by the heat when you roast the bird but can linger on your chopping board and your hands if you do not wash everything you use in preparation carefully.

There are lots of things you can do to change the taste of your chicken. We are going to take the simplest way to roast it and then you can start experimenting to find your favourite.

Turn the oven on to medium, about 160-180. Get a baking tray ready and oil the bottom or rub the tray with butter paper. Use just enough so that the bird won't stick. Take the bird out of the wrapper and put it in the tray. Write down the weight of the bird before you throw away the wrapper. You don't need to wash the bird, but you can rub it with a paper towel inside and out if it needs it. I like to cut the elastic now so that the heat can get between its legs and reach its breast. Rub the breast and legs with a little oil or butter and you are ready for the oven.

You now need to do a little maths. The chicken needs 15 minutes for each pound and an extra 15 minutes for the bird, so if it weighs three pounds it will need an hour. So you multiply the weight by 15 minutes for the length of time in minutes to cook the bird.

After 15 or 20 minutes, take the chicken out and spoon the juices from the bottom of the tray over the bird to baste it. You may need to tip the tray a bit so the juices run out of the parson's nose. Do this every 15 minutes until the time is up. When the time is up you have to put the bird onto a plate and rest it for another 15 minutes before you carve it up and eat it. Don't take the word of the supplier on the weight of the bird. They often weigh the bird before it is dressed for the oven, with its head, feet and innards intact, so your 7lb bird may only weigh 6lbs oven ready. This is why people often end up with a very dry, overcooked bird.

What to do with a broiler (boiling hen)

Our basic method works OK for chickens you buy. The chickens we buy to roast are really only babies and have certainly not been allowed to exercise. The chickens you eat from the yard will need more care if they are to be tender and juicy. This is because they have had a good life, they have had lots of exercise and lived more than a few weeks. Mostly they are quite old and have finished laying and brooding. They need long, slow cooking. You can still do things like fried chicken, but you need to boil them slowly for 2 or 3 hours with carrot, onion and celery before you cook them in your favourite way. Or you can casserole them and add flavour with lemons and herbs. Keep the stock you have made in the boiling for soups, stews and risottos.

Fried chicken

When you have boiled a chicken and let it get cold, you can do many things. This is an old favourite in our house. Cut off the legs and cut into a thigh and a drumstick. Cut off the wings and take off the tiny end of the wings. You now have 6 pieces of chicken. Crack an egg into a bowl and beat. Half fill another bowl with bread crumbs you have made from crusts. Now flavour the crumbs with any herbs and spices you. You can buy all sorts of mixes like barbecue, garam masala or cajun. It's good fun to invent your own, you could become famous like Kentucky Fried Chicken.

Dust the chicken pieces with a little flour and put them one at a time into the beaten egg with your right hand and drop them in the breadcrumbs. With your left hand turn them over and over until they are covered in crumbs. Do this with all the chicken pieces and leave them to stand in the fridge until you are ready to fry. You can fry them in the chip pan but they do mess up the oil. Best to put some oil in a deep frying pan and fry until they are as golden and crisp as you like them. They don't need long because the chicken is already cooked.

Chicken pie

You will have 2 breasts left on the carcass. These are delicious in a pie if you help them along with a tin of condensed chicken soup and a tin of sweetcorn. Chop up the chicken and put in a pie dish with the soup, the corn and herbs you like. Tarragon is my favourite. Mix it all up. Cut a sheet of ready-rolled pastry to size and cook until the pastry is golden. It won't take long because everything is cooked but the pastry. You can experiment with the left-over pastry as we did earlier.

Break the remaining carcass up and put it back in the stock with 2 chicken stock cubes and a glass of white wine, if you have any going begging. Simmer gently for 15 minutes and then strain through a sieve. Chop up your favourite vegetables and add to the stock and cook until they are tender. Thicken the soup with left over mashed potatoes or cornflour and serve with crusty bread. If you use tomatoes to thicken instead, with broken-up spaghetti, and add Italian herbs, you have a sort of minestrone.

Now for some very grown-up cooking.

Lemon chicken – a very fattening, yummy treat

Ingredients

1 large broiler
8 shallots
8 ounces carrots
4 ounces mushrooms
1 green pepper
4 ounces cashew nuts
3 bay leaves
4 tbs cream
1 lemon
1 egg
2 ounces butter
Glass of sherry

Method

Clean the bird and place in a casserole dish or pressure cooker. Cut the lemon in half and squeeze the juice onto the breast of the bird. Put the remains of the lemon into the cavity with the bay leaves. Scatter the chopped carrots, shallots and pepper around the bird, then cover with water and season with lashings of white and black pepper. Cover and place in a slow oven for 3 to 4 hours or pressure cook for 30 minutes. When tender, remove the chicken from the stock and leave to rest on a serving dish.

Fry the mushrooms in butter. Whip the egg and cream and gradually add a mug of the hot stock. Slowly add the sherry, then add the nuts and mushrooms. Pour the sauce around the bird and serve immediately with jacket potatoes and crisp salad.

Chapter Six

Cooking your Christmas capon

A capon is a cockerel that has been neutered so he can't have babies, just as we do to a male cat to stop him stinking the house out with his wee. This makes them grow much bigger faster so he won't be as tough as an old bird. You can usually buy capons at Xmas at proper butchers. Don't take the word of the supplier on the weight of the bird – they often weigh the bird before it is dressed for the oven, with its head, feet and innards intact. So your 7 lb bird may only weigh 6lbs oven ready. This is why people often end up with a very dry, overcooked bird for Christmas dinner.

Ingredients

One large capon
2 small onions
tbsp sage
4 ounces butter
8 slices of streaky bacon
2 pounds of thin sausages

Method

Clean and dry the bird and place in a lightly greased baking tin. Peel the onions and place in the cavity. Very carefully push your fingers between the skin and the breast. Smooth the butter and mix in the sage. Now put this mixture under the breast skin, making sure to cover both breasts well.

Remove any rind from the bacon and put it in a criss-cross pattern over the breast, making sure that the entire breast is covered.

Place in a medium oven for 15 minutes for the bird and a further 15 minutes for each pound the bird weighs. You will hear when the fat starts to flow; spoon this fat over the bird every 30 minutes or so, taking care not to dislodge the bacon coat. Add the sausages 20 minutes before the bird is due out or when you open the oven to put on the Yorkshire Pudding. Serve with your preferred Xmas fare.

Research
Finding out about which chickens you can buy

Next time you go to the supermarket with the children, take a note book with you and find out:

How many different sizes of chickens do they have?

What are they called?

Do they have spatchcock chickens?

Do they have poussins?

Do they sell chicken cut up into pieces like drumsticks, thighs, breasts?

Can you buy chicken that is fresh or frozen?

Which chicken do you think is the best value?

Remember we said that happy hens lay better eggs. Do you think that happy hens also make good eating?

What sort of hens do you think go into things like chicken nuggets or chicken goujons?

Experiment with blowing eggs

We are going to blow the inside out of an egg so that we can paint and decorate the shell for a Christmas present for someone you love. If you wash your hands before we start, you can keep the eggshell contents to make batter or omelettes.

Begin by finding a perfectly-shaped egg. You may not have noticed until now that they do vary in shape quite a bit. You will need a bowl, an egg cup and a long darning needle. If

Chapter Six

you are saving the egg, you will need to sterilise the needle with boiling water or a gas flame. Put the egg in an egg cup with its flattest side uppermost. Now gently tap at the top of the egg in the same spot until a hole is made. Make this hole a little bigger. Push the needle all the way into the egg to break the yolk. Now turn the egg over and do the same to the other end.

Now, holding the egg over a bowl, very gently blow into the smallest hole and some of the egg white should come out of the larger hole. Keep blowing until all the egg is out of the shell. Now wipe the egg clean and put it somewhere to dry out on the inside. Be careful to wipe off all the egg white, because it sets like glue. We once put all our eggs on the window sill to dry overnight. In the morning they were all stuck in a row along the window sill and broke when we tried to move them.

When you have a dried egg shell you can decorate it any way you like – paint, sequins, beads, dried flowers, chocolate wrappers, food dye, ribbons. Phew, anything. Remember the eggshell is porous so water paint is not so good.

You can blow all types of eggs. Big goose eggs are fantastic to work with.

Chapter Eight

Indian Runners

Chapter Eight

Indian Runner ducks were found in Java up to a thousand years or so ago. Explorers liked the way they stood so tall and "walked erect, like penguins". They are lovely tall upright ducks with elegant bodies. Not for these graceful creatures a duck waddle across the yard. They were first called penguin ducks. Unlike most other ducks they are flightless and can run extremely fast. They also lay lots beautiful eggs and grow rapidly. They are also extremely funny to watch, especially when they are in love.

If you like eating duck eggs, female Indian Runner ducks are fabulous layers but not good broodies. Anyone wishing to hatch out Indian Runner eggs who also keeps chickens would do well to use a broody hen.

Indian Runners in the yard

You can see why the Indian Runner was the breed of choice when Keeper's wife was considering expanding the egg industry to duck eggs. These ducks are very good layers, the eggs are delicious and they make reasonably good table birds, reaching about 4 pounds, although they do not really have the shape for it. They have long, sleek bodies and really are more like a penguin than a

Indian Runners

duck. Their tail is a funny little thing with a curl and they tuck their wings tightly over their backs, emphasising their long thin bodies. The fact that they are not good at brooding their eggs is not too off putting, because we know what fun it can be watching a broody hen rearing ducklings.

One day in the spring, a box of ducklings arrived. They were only a day old and were destined to be reared in an incubator. They were quite pricey, but Keeper's wife was optimistic that they would quickly pay her back. She devoted watchful, loving care on them, as you do any investment, and they grew and grew. Eventually they were turned loose in the yard, as the policy was free range even if the birds had cost a bit. The problem now was catching the little beggars when they needed handling for some reason.

Indian Runners really are the comedians of the duck world. They like to live in herds and hang around together like sheep. They go everywhere at top speed and could never be accused of waddling. When going down to the pond they approach the steep bank on their chest, flattening themselves to the muddy ground and sliding in like a penguin on an ice pack, usually all at once, landing with plop, plop, plop into the water. As a consequence the runners were never really white in our yard.

Naughty boys and spotty ducks

The problem of their speed became apparent when they appeared one day all covered in reddish coloured spots. They looked for all the world as if they had chicken pox. I knew they lived in close proximity to the chickens but even chickens don't get chicken pox. The family were summoned and all came to help except Oldest Son and his friend, who were out somewhere with their airguns.

The chase began focusing first on the most serious case of spots. Unfortunately, this one seemed to be the most nervous of the lot and she legged it the minute anyone got close. Eventually the ducks were driven into the stables, which made them easier to catch. On inspection the spots were only feather deep with no evidence of torn flesh or injury. They seemed to be paint or dye or something. Anyway the ducks were fine, if a little more skittish than usual.

That evening when Keeper's wife went to get the washing off the line she found to her chagrin that the laundry seemed to also be suffering from the same mystery disease as the ducks. This coincided with the appearance of two young men with purple-stained fingers and air guns. Duck everybody, big trouble ahead. Children were not 'grounded' in 1975, but there were lots of stables that needed cleaning out and lots of manure to shift.

They had discovered that elderberries make fantastic substitutes for air gun pellets. They are free, don't kill what they hit and are an excellent way of getting your eye in and sighting your gun as you can see quite clearly when you score a hit.

Double trouble for the boys. When Keeper came home he found his white van was also covered in little red spots. Van cleaning then after mucking out the stables. A long night ahead for the two trainee marksmen.

Duck eggs

We know already that chicken eggs from the yard are 10 times better than the insipid mellow yolks and sloppy whites of a supermarket egg. Duck eggs are even better, with a rich smooth orange yolk and very solid white. Duck eggs are far superior to chicken eggs, with a stronger taste and richer, smoother consistency. They have lots of other things going for them too. They stay fresh for longer and make cakes spongier and Yorkshire puddings taller. They are best for breakfast eaten boiled or poached rather than part of another recipe. You can use them in almost any recipe except meringue, as the whites are the devil to whisk.

Some people say it is as good for you to eat an egg a day as it is to eat an apple. Duck eggs are alkaline and so make your body more alkaline, which is great for cancer patients as cancer cells do not thrive in an alkaline environment. Chicken eggs are more acid.

There are two reasons given why you should not eat duck eggs. The first is the old myth that they are

Indian Runners

poisonous and upset your tummy. This probably stems back to the days when we were less hygienic in our egg sheds. We now know that egg shells are porous and so we prevent rodents from running over our trays of eggs, tiddling as they go. We also wipe the eggs clean when we collect them. Another thing more worrying is the claim that they increase cholesterol in the blood. I'm not qualified to advise on the veracity of this statement as I don't really understand the difference between good cholesterol and bad. Don't pig out on any one thing is my philosophy, and run around every day after your Indian Runners.

Chapter Eight

Yum-Yum Corner
Roast duck

Assuming they arrive in your kitchen oven ready, you simply roast them in your preferred way, giving about 12 minutes per pound and 12 minutes for the bird. So a 3lb bird will want about 48 minutes. If you like your duck a little more well done, add a couple of minutes per pound. Be careful though – the best way to ruin a duck is to overcook it. For a lovely golden shine brush the duck with a mix of 1 tsp honey and 1 tsp hot water 15 minute before the end of the cooking time.

Indian Runners

Crispy Fried Duck with Pancakes

Ingredients
1 Roasted Duck,
2 legs and 2 breasts

Pancake Batter
1 mug of plain flour
2 eggs
1 mug of milk
Pinch of salt

Method

Take the breasts and legs off your roasted duck and reserve the bones for stock. Remove the skins from the breasts and legs and thinly slice them. Place these skin slices in a dry pan and put on a low heat to render out the grease. When the slices are crisp and well fried remove and drain on kitchen paper. Save the fat. Thinly slice the duck breasts and legs and toss the slices in a little seasoned flour. Add these to the very hot fat left by the skins. When crisp remove and drain on kitchen paper.

To make the pancake batter simply put all the ingredients in a bowl and whisk until smooth and the consistency of pouring cream. Add a little iced water if your batter is too thick. It can differ with the size of your eggs and the type of flour you use.

Heat a solid frying pan, add a tiny amount of the duck fat, just enough to cover the pan, when this is smoking hot add a sauce ladle of the batter and swish it about to form a thin layer in the pan. It will be cooked almost as soon as it hits the pan if you have the pan hot enough and don't put in too much batter. Now either toss it or turn it with a fish slice to cook the other side and turn out onto a heatproof dish covered in paper towel. Don't worry if the first one is a disaster, it nearly always takes one or two to get the pan used to the job in hand. Keep going until you have used up all the batter. Now spread each pancake with your favourite sauce, plum is good, as is bramble or crab apple jelly, pear pickle is awesome. You would have all of these in your pantry if you are a good country woman. Now fill with crispy duck and prepare to go to heaven.

If you eat green things you could add lettuce and spring onions.

Chapter Eight

Research
Finding out about ducks for roasting

Next time you and the children go to the supermarket, take your notebook with you. Take a good look at the ducks on the shelves, at the butchers and in the freezers.

How many different kinds of ducks do they have?

How many different sizes of ducks do they have? Are there really small ones like the little poussin chickens?

What are they called?

Can you buy duck portions, legs and breasts, as well as whole ducks?

Which duck would you buy?

Conclusions……………………………………………………………………………
………………………………………………………………………………………
………………………………………………………………………………………
………………………………………………………………………………………
………………………………………………………………………………………
………………………………………………………………………………………
………………………………………………………………………………………
………………………………………………………………………………………
………………………………………………………………………………………
………………………………………………………………………………………

Indian Runners

Experiment: Observation of a Duck pond

Take your notebook along to a duck pond and carry out an observation of the ducks for 15 minutes. When we carry out an observation it is best to make an observation sheet rather than just sit and write things down. This helps us record more accurately and not miss behaviour while we are writing. This one might do:

	Swimming	Preening	Eating	Fighting	Mating	Other
1 min						
2 min						
3 mins						
4 mins						
5 mins						
10 mins						
15 mins						

You just need to tick in the boxes and analyse when you get home.

Chapter Eight

Making a nest

While you are at the pond, look at the possible nesting material. Gather together things that you think might make a nest. When you get home see if you can make a nest that would hold a clutch of eggs. Hint: you might want to use mud to stick it all together.

The Ugly Duckling

Early one spring, baby ducks hatched
Mother was so proud, yet one didn't match
Brother and sister soon started to tease,
Strutting about with the greatest of ease.
Your friends call you ugly, ugly by name.
They laugh and they gawk, they point and they blame,
Calling Ugly Ooo Ooo Ooo,
I'm glad I'm not you, ugly you!
It's a pity, such a shame, when looks are not the same
and you're called ugly Ooo Ooo Ooo.

Oh, It's hard to listen when the words are so mean
How can friends cause such a scene?
Acting so important while being so bad,
not even caring that others are sad.
It's a pity, such a shame, when looks are not the same
and you're called ugly Ooo Ooo Ooo.
So your feathers aren't sparkly with a colourful sheen,
You're such a good swimmer you could be queen.
Swimming circles around the rest.

Indian Runners

You're kind and sincere, who cares who looks best?
You're not ugly -- you're unique, just wait one day you'll
see, that your not ugly Ooo Ooo Ooo.

Sure enough it happened, the very next spring,
The water reflected such a beautiful thing
Swimming about, could it really be true?
The prettiest image, how could it be you?
Your no duckling, you're a swan. You've been one all
along and you're not ugly Ooo Ooo Ooo.
So try not to listen when others are mean,
Trying to look big and causing a scene.
Being a bully is never cool,
sooner or later you'll look like a fool.
Sure looks they may fade, but to friends you're never strange
Yeah looks they may fade, but good friends will stay.
And you'll never be ugly, Ooo Ooo Ooo.

Chapter Nine

Becoming a duck owner

The arrival of 27 Muscovies

One day in summer, the farmer's boy turned up with a tractor and a trailer full of Muscovy ducks. His Mum had put up with a huge quantity of ducks and the mess they make and had given him final warning that they must go. He was supposed to put them in the freezer, but instead he piled them all in the trailer and donated them to the Keeper's yard. Most of the stock arrived like this. Other people would acquire things like a billy goat or two or three nanny goats, which would then start destroying the environment and would have to be re-homed.

To return to the Muscovies, when the tarpaulin was taken off the trailer it revealed a scruffy mix of different-coloured ducks, mostly black and white but some lovely lavender-coloured ones. Lots of them had huge red lumps above their beaks. They seemed to be mostly drakes which began making an awful din, laughing at us and wheezing like heavy smokers at the end of a night's boozing. They were all filthy dirty and looked very thin. It was tempting to just turn them out and let them at the pond, but Keeper's wife knew they would be very hard to catch once set free.

Taking control, she told threw the boy a sack or two and told him to bag up the ones that looked like drakes

Chapter Nine

and chuck the females at the pond whilst she went off and prepared accommodation for the drakes. She ended up with five sacks of drakes and seven girls set free.

She chucked some corn out round the pond for the girls and soaked a bucket of corn in very hot water to feed to the drakes later.

She set about assessing the boys. She quickly learnt that the body language of drakes can seem quite threatening but doesn't necessarily mean they are about to attack. If he comes straight at you with his head down and wings spread out, he means to have you. If he comes at you with his beak open and hissing his throaty 'ha ha', bobbing his head up and down and wagging his tail, then he means no harm.

Keeper's wife left them for an hour or so to settle down and then took the bucket of soaked grain into the stables. Whilst they were tucking in she could weigh them up and decide what to do with them. The first thing to do was decide which of the 20 were going to join the girls at the pond. Small son was perched on a barrel giving advice and choosing which boys he wanted to keep. Eventually he decided on a very big, black drake with the loudest 'he he' cough. The second one was a beautiful lavender and white drake who was almost as big as the first one chosen. These were to become Blackie and Pinky. Very original. They were allowed to join the girls on the pond, who were now making a tremendous din splashing, running and wing flapping across the water. Finally, taking a break, my word they look happy.

Leaving the boy parked in his toy jeep watching the antics of the new arrivals, Keeper's wife returned to the stable to make decisions. 18 drakes left. A few seemed quite plump, while others were terrible scrawny. The question was whether it was worth trying to fatten up the scrawny ones. OK, be bold. Six plumpish drakes go into the freezer now and 12 go into the laying pen just vacated by new-released hen pheasants to be fattened. Problem solved.

Learning about ducks

This is how Keeper's wife began to

learn about proper ducks. They are very different from chickens in many ways. The first big difference is that ducks exist in the wild, so it's not impossible to find a mother mallard joining all the Muscovies and Indians on the pond. Once they knew the routine they would turn up for breakfast when Keeper's wife did the 'chuck, chuck, chuck' that meant food time in the yard. They are very engaging to see bobbing about on the water. Indeed it is a favourite pastime in Britain to feed ducks on a pond. Unfortunately people usually feed bread, which is very bad for ducks, especially growing ones. I know you can get corn-fed chicken, but whoever bought bread-fed duck?

Thinking of the pond brings me onto the next big difference. Ducks love water and will happily dibble about in anything that looks like water, even the septic tank (this is where the sewage goes for lots of country folk). You don't need a pond to keep ducks, but they will find water in the daftest places and they will swim off down the stream if you have one at the bottom of your garden. They are also very, very messy. They poo at least 30 times a day.

Fertilising the garden

They do have their good points though. They fertilise the garden continuously, they give organic fertiliser wherever they go and are brilliant at pest control. They particularly love slugs and snails and turn this natural diet into fantastic eggs with bright yellow yolks.

As the pond ducks grew more adventurous, they showed that they were very good woodland ducks. They could perch in a tree at night and keep themselves safe from foxes. Ducks have little claws on their webbed feet that they can hook into bark. They also took to roosting on the roof of the stables and goat sheds. This could be quite dangerous for the passer-by as they came down from roost in the morning. Their mid-flight aim wasn't very good. They flipping hurt when they collided with you as they veered to the left and then to the right. Yet another obstacle to dodge between the house and the car when getting kids off on the school run.

Chapter Nine

They are very social birds and will run at you when you arrive home at night, always in a group. The children soon learned not to stand in the way if they were in low flight coming at you. Not only was their 'in flight' steering rubbish, their brakes weren't brilliant either.

Ducks in the snow

They were at their funniest when there was frost and snow. Their flat, webbed feet were really bad at getting a grip of the frozen ground. They would slide down the bank of the pond, not able to slow themselves down, but expecting to plop into the water when they reached the bottom. Instead they would end up whirling round and round on the ice with legs slipping out from under them and wings flapping trying to get a balance.

Even funnier was when they decided to fly down to the pond. Expecting to land in water, they would hit the ice a high speed and whirl around the pond, unable to control anything until they hit the bank somewhere. Six or seven arriving at one time is the greatest thing to watch ever.

Like the hens, they liked to help in the yard and garden. They would follow the lawn mower and clean up any bits of chopped-up insect or dead animal that might have been caught by the mower, including rats. Amazingly ducks turn all this pest control and foraging into eggs that we can sell and eat. Another blessing is that they rear their own ducklings, supplying new ducks for the yard next year and young drakes for the pot.

Yum-Yum Corner
Roast duckling and orange sauce

At eight weeks old, Muscovy ducklings are the perfect shape for roasting. Assuming they arrive in your kitchen oven ready, you simply roast them in your preferred way, giving about 12 minutes per pound and 12 minutes for the bird, so a 4lb bird will want about an hour. If you like your duck a little more well done, add a couple of minutes per pound. Be careful though, the best way to ruin a duck is to overcook it. For a lovely golden shine brush the duck with a mix of 1 tsp honey and 1 tsp hot water 15 minute before the end of the cooking time.

Orange Sauce

Ingredients:

3 oranges
The giblets
One small onion
2 small carrots
Large glass of port
1 pint of stock

The sauce

Take the zest off the oranges with a zester, taking care not to dig deeply into the pith. Squeeze the juice out of one of the oranges into the liquor and add the port. Simmer this to reduce, tasting from time to time. When it reaches the consistency and depth of flavour you want, season and pour into a sauce boat. Cut the remaining oranges into thin slices and use to garnish the duck.

Place the cleaned giblets in a pan with the peeled and chopped onion and carrots. Cover with water, add a teaspoon of Marmite and simmer for an hour.

Strain the liquor and put the cooked giblets to one side for soup or pasties.

This duck goes very well with rice or vegetables.

Chapter Nine

Duck breast and new vegetables (an August feast)

If you are lucky, your ducks will be ready at the same time as early carrots, peas, runner beans and new potatoes. All of this produce fresh from the garden is to die for. The key here is to keep all the cooking to a minimum and just savour the tastes. You will need one duck between two and as much veg as you know your family will eat.

The vegetables

Boil the potatoes and carrots in lightly salted water and steam the other vegetables in a colander over the potatoes. Toss all the vegetables in a little butter and freshly-chopped mint before serving.

The duck

Remove the breasts by first slicing into the breast by the wing so that the bottom of the breast is not attached to the carcass. Then run a sharp knife down the breastbone centre and feel your way along the bone until the breast comes free. Put the remainder of the duck to one side for other dishes.

Now lay the breast skin up on the chopping board and cut a criss-cross pattern in the skin of each one. Heat a heavy frying pan, but add no fat. When smoking hot, place the duck breasts into the pan skin down. Turn down the heat and cook gently for about 10 minutes until the cooked edge of the breast nearly reaches the top of the portion. Now drain off all the fat that has come out of the breasts into a basin and keep it for roasting potatoes. Turn the breast to cook the underside for a minute or two.

Remove from the heat and serve with the fresh vegetables. A little crab apple jelly gives the meal a luxurious finish.

Crispy duck legs and roast potatoes

Ingredients:

1 leg per person

1 large or 2 small potatoes per person

2 ounces of seasoned flour

Hoi-sin sauce

Green salad

The duck

Remove the legs from the carcasses of the ducks. Dry them with a paper towel and dust them with seasoned flour all over.

Brush a roasting tin with a little of the saved fat and add the legs and chopped-up carcass. Put into a very hot oven for about 30 minutes, depending on the size of the legs. They are done when the skin of the legs is dark and crispy.

The potatoes

Peel the potatoes and chop into equal sizes. Boil them in salted water until they are looking fluffy. Heat some of the duck fat in the oven until it is smoking. Put the potatoes in at 180° for about 20 minutes or until golden brown.

Pull the leg meat off the bones and serve with the roast potatoes, Hoi-sin Sauce and a crispy green salad.

Chapter Nine

Duck risotto

Roast the carcasses as you cook the legs. The following day, break the carcasses into pieces and place in a large pan or pressure cooker with the giblets, an onion, carrot and Italian seasoning and pint of water. Use the water to deglaze the roasting dish. All those little bits that look burnt will add loads of flavour to your dish. A glass of Chianti is also good here. The rule is one for the pot, one for the chef. Season with salt and black pepper. Simmer gently on the back of the stove for about an hour or pressure cook for 15 minutes. Strain off the liquor and reserve.

When the bones are cool, pick off any remaining meat and add to the chopped giblets. Discard the bones.

The risotto

Begin by putting your rich stock on to heat through. For every cup of rice you will need about 2 cups of stock. Use good risotto rice, like Arborio. Long grain rice or paella rice won't work. Put a little duck fat in a heavy pan to heat with a good spoonful of Italian herbs and toss in the rice to start to cook it. Stir all the time. Risotto rice gets lonely if you leave it and will not be as nice. When it begins to stick to the pan add a ladle of the hot stock. The stirring helps break the rice down and stops it burning. Just when you think it is beginning to burn, put in another ladle of stock. Keep doing this until all the stock is used up. Stir all the time. Season with salt and pepper if it needs it. Sometimes the stock was enough seasoning. Add the bits of cooked meat at the end of the cooking time.

There is much debate about how well-cooked the rice should be. Some people like it a little hard, to the tooth, but not chalky. Some people like it wet and sloppy. Some people like it cooked well and sticking together in a clump. You need to experiment to see how you like it best. You can add grated parmesan cheese at the end. Some people add cream.

Serve with a cool cucumber salad.

Mallard and other wild ducks

Mallard are very small in comparison to domestic ducks. If you can buy them in your butchers they are probably the result of a wildfowling trip and will have been shot. This means that you have no way of knowing how old or how tough they are. Because of this it is best to use a slow cooking method. You also don't know how long they have been dead (called 'hanging'), so they may be very gamey.

Devilled duck

Ingredients:

1 duck per person
For each duck take
1 oz. of streaky bacon
1 small onion
1 small carrot
1 stick of celery
1lb mashed potatoes
½ mug stock
2 oz. plain flour
2 oz. butter
2 tsp mustard

Method

Clean and dry the duck. Wrap the peeled onion in a rasher of streaky bacon and insert into the duck cavity. Place all the ducks in a casserole dish and add the chopped carrots and celery

The stock for two birds

Crumble a stock cube into a mug of water and add a tsp. of mustard powder and season to taste with salt and pepper. Use less mustard if you like your devils a little less hot. It is always possible to add more heat, but you can't take it out once it's in.

Pour this over the ducks. Seal the dish with a lid and place in a medium oven for about 90 minutes. Meanwhile prepare the mashed potatoes.

When the duck is cooked strain off the liquor into a jug and remove the onion and bacon from inside the bird.

Chapter Nine

Melt the butter in a heavy pan and stir in the flour. Gradually add the liquor to the sauce and cook until smooth stirring all the time. Check for seasoning.

Place one duck on a dinner plate along with its onion and share of the vegetables and spoon over some of the sauce. Pipe a border of mashed potato around the duck and vegetables and serve immediately.

Research
Finding out about potatoes for roasting

Next time you go to the supermarket with the children, take your notebook with you. Take a good look at the potatoes. You have probably found a confusing array of different potatoes. It helps to divide them up into different types.

The first big division is between new and old potatoes. New potatoes are usually smaller and have loose skin. These are best boiled, covered in butter with salt and black pepper.

How many types of new potato can you spot?

Old potatoes can be divided in two main ways. These are red and white. Another division is floury and waxy potatoes. Both reds and whites can be all-purpose potatoes and good for boiling, roasting, baking and salads, so it's not so much the colour that is important.

How many types of old potato can you spot?

The floury, waxy dimension is more important. Floury potatoes fall apart in the cooking but waxy potatoes hold the shape.

Can you tell from the labelling which are floury potatoes and which are waxy?

Can you find King Edward potatoes or Desiree? These are floury or fluffy potatoes. Good for roasting.

Can you find potatoes that are good for baking in the jacket? Usually the only special purpose potato sold in supermarkets.

Conclusions……………………………………………………………………………
…………………………………………………………………………………………
…………………………………………………………………………………………
…………………………………………………………………………………………
…………………………………………………………………………………………
…………………………………………………………………………………………
…………………………………………………………………………………………
…………………………………………………………………………………………
…………………………………………………………………………………………

Potato Experiment: A piece of long term research

Over the next few weeks buy the smallest available amount of each type of potato. When your collection is complete, boil them all in unsalted water until soft to the tip of a knife. Mash them, but do not add anything until after your tasting. Taste and rate the potatoes on a scale of 1 to 10 in terms of fluffiness, taste, texture, so each potato gets a possible score of 30. Write a report on each one that will help you identify your preferred potato for the future.

Chapter Ten

Barney and the ganders

Back to fostering: a sad tale

SPECIES	INCUBATION PERIOD
Chickens	24 Days
Bantams	21 Days
Partridges	21 Days
Pheasants	24 Days
Ducks	28 Days
Muscovy	35-37 Days
Geese	28-30 Days
Swans	30-37 Days

Things to consider before cross-fostering

The first important thing to know is how long eggs take to hatch. As you can see, they all have different incubation periods. For this reason it is best not to mix species when using a foster mother. Another thing is that the shells of species are different. Pigeon eggshells are very thin, whilst those of geese are thick. Hens turn the eggs over every day. This stops the chick getting stuck to the inside of the eggshell. If the broody has large clumsy feet she will smash the eggs.

There is a membrane between the egg and the shell that you will have seen when you are peeling hard boiled eggs. Water birds like ducks and geese get wet every day when they leave the nest to eat and poo. When they get back to the nest they dampen everything so that the eggs stay moist. This increases the humidity and helps the chick develop and eventually hatch. If the eggs are too dry the membrane will become rubbery and the chick will not be able to break through the shell. If you have to use a chicken to hatch duck eggs, you need to spray them with water mist every day.

Lastly, different chicks require different food when they hatch. Crucial to remember this as you will see when we see what happened to Barney's first brood.

Chapter Ten

A very confused goose

One day in November a big white goose called Barney arrived in the yard to act as a guard dog. Geese are very noisy creatures who hate to be disturbed by people or foxes arriving, particularly at night. Barney was magnificent. He honked loudly and ran at intruders with his neck stretched out, chasing even the boldest visitor away. The whole winter passed by without a single chicken being taken by foxes. Barney made a din so loud that it even woke the gamekeeper when there were foxes about.

When the spring came Barney had a couple of surprises for Keeper and his wife. Firstly, he was a fabulous lawn mower, eating grass all day. He also laid an egg, so he was a goose, not a gander. He laid another, and another. These were infertile of course, because Barney did not have a mate. They were delicious however and just the thing for the children at Easter, although they were huge. They needed to be boiled for twenty minutes and it took an entire loaf for dippy soldiers. This wouldn't be nice for Barney when she went broody.

Barney spent a second winter in the yard guarding the poultry. When spring came again she once again started laying her lovely big white eggs. She was by now recognised as a female, but hung onto her rather masculine name. She laid and laid and laid. Each time Little Son stole a goose egg he replaced it with one stolen from a Muscovy duck. The question was – would she be able to foster ducklings?

Hatching across species

If eggs are to hatch they need heat and humidity (moistness). When hatching across species, for example asking a goose to hatch duck eggs, you need to be sure that your foster mother will provide both of these adequately. For example, the ideal temperature for a goose egg is 99 degrees and a humidity count of 86-88, whereas for a duck it is 100 degrees and 85-86 humidity. All species need increased humidity in the last few days of incubation if they are to hatch successfully, for example a pheasant needs a humidity count of

92 if it is not to get stuck to the inside of the shell. Sorry, am I boring you?

Each species also has a different incubation period. Usually, the bigger the egg the longer the incubation. For example a quail or pigeon will hatch in 17 days, as will some small bantams, whereas a chicken takes about 21 days. Pheasants on the other hand are more unpredictable, taking between 23 and 28 days. Geese take 28-34 days and Muscovy ducks 35-37. It is therefore best to stick to hatching within species, or do it in an incubator if the eggs are very precious.

If you are to offer a goose Muscovy duck eggs therefore, you should consider the following. The eggs will take longer than the goose is programmed to sit for, so she may stand up 9 days before the eggs hatch. She will not keep the eggs at 100 degrees and she will provide slightly more humidity than they need.

So would Barney be able to hatch duck eggs? As the species were so close she ought to be able to do so. They were about half the size hers would be but had very tough shells. She would also keep up the humidity in the nest after her daily swim, so she would certainly be a better foster mother for the duckling than a chicken would.

She got to 18 eggs and stopped, seeming to ignore the nest of eggs.

Then another arrived, then another and another. These were infertile of course, because Barney still didn't have a mate. They were delicious however and there was such a glut of them that year that Keeper's wife began trying all sorts of recipes to see how they worked best.

Chapter Ten

A broody goose

When Barney finally went broody, Keeper's wife sorted out the duck eggs, taking away the ones that looked old and tired. She had no idea how long the eggs had been laid or who Little Son had stolen them from, and some of them looked more than a little seedy.

Barney did an excellent job with the 10 eggs left. Even though the eggs were a little small for a goose they were quite large for a duck, and took 35 days to hatch. When they hatched the chicks did quite well for a few days, although they were a very strange colour for goslings. Barney took them to the pond and got them swimming. She spent hours blissfully circling the pond with her brood of babies on her back.

Problems began for Barney and the ducklings when she tried to get them to eat grass. Goslings of course love grass and will happily spend all day mowing the lawn for you. These weird goslings however seemed more interested in the things flying in the air and wriggling on the ground. Barney would pull frantically at the grass, showing her youngsters how to eat it. They would watch her with stupid looks on their faces and peep until she became very frustrated and reverted to brooding behaviour, which seemed to be all her kids were good at. She was a very disappointed mother.

The ducklings failed to thrive and didn't grow very well. They began to look quite ill. After finding two dead, emaciated little bodies Keeper's wife realised that they were not eating properly. We hadn't taken into account the different diets. These babies may have been better with a chicken after all. So she began giving them duckling food while Barney was eating grass. They soon grew into strong, healthy ducks.

This just goes to show that you need to eat proper food for your own species to grow big and strong and sometimes worms and grubs are better than roast beef and Yorkshire pudding and certainly better than grass.

Barney's new mate

After another year of guarding through the winter and one warm day in May a handsome gander arrived in the yard. He was to be a

Barney and the ganders

mate for Barney so that this year she could have real goslings. He was grey and striped and called a Toulouse goose. He was magnificent as he strutted about the yard.

He was a little odd, however. Every time the children played football he tried to join in. He ran after the ball with his neck stretched out, making a very silly peeping sound. If he found the ball abandoned in the yard after the game, he would try to climb onto it. He looked very odd with his big pink feet sticking out between him and the football.

Soon after he arrived, Barney began to follow him around. She would preen his neck and eyes and twirl her neck around him lovingly. He did not seem to like her very much and nobody ever saw him mating with her. She began to lay eggs and eventually went broody. She sat on the eggs for nearly two months, but no goslings appeared.

One day there was a huge bang and a very nasty smell came from under Barney. Her eggs were not fertile and had gone rotten while she sat on them. They were now exploding because they were filled with gas. Nobody was brave enough to lift Barney off the eggs. She was very vicious when protecting her eggs, and boy did she smell. After a while she left the smelly mess and went for a nice swim in the pond.

Learning about imprinting

Well, what do you think happened? Did Barney's new mate not mate with her? Did he mate with the football? Did something happen to him when he was a baby to make him think he was a football? Maybe the first moving thing he saw was a football and he imprinted on it and has been in love with them ever since.

Imprinting is nature's glue. It sticks the babies to their mum. Chicks that are mobile as soon as they hatch are called 'gallinaceous species'. They are biologically programmed to follow the first moving thing they see. There are some very famous studies of imprinting. The most famous pioneer

Chapter Ten

in this field was a man called Lorenz. He went so far as to swim in the lake with goslings that had imprinted on him.

So what do we do with a posh Toulouse gander that will only mate with a football?

Barney and George: love at last

At last, a gander with lead in his pencil. The minute George arrived he took over the yard. Chickens, ducks and guinea fowl all beat a hasty retreat when George passed by. He was first at the morning corn, always taking more than his share. He was first on the scene when visitors arrived, not stopping at honking and neck plunging did but getting involved in actual bodily harm. He quickly earned the respect of birds, animals and children, all of whom exhibited mortal fear when he approached. Even the billy goat kept his distance.

Barney and George made a handsome couple, she serene in her new-found love life and he grand in his command of all he surveyed. He was handsome and admired himself hugely in the shiny hubcap of the car

– or was this honking and pecking at the hubcap a sign that he thought his refection was the face of a rival?

That year Barney hatched actual, real goslings. They were beautiful, fluffy and yellow and full of life. Their collective mission seemed to be to eat as much grass and as many flowers as possible. They loved the water and used either George or Barney to hitch a ride whenever they were tired of swimming. Barney had never seemed more content.

George, on the other hand, got even more vicious, attacking everyone who went near the gosling or anywhere else in the yard that he thought he owned. The children were terrified of him and could not go out to play without being attacked and hissed at.

The madness of a gander

In fact he was becoming quite psychotic, if that is possible for a gander, even going so far as to attach Keeper's wife when she went to the store for corn, leaving a series of purple bruises all down the calf of her right leg.

She was now caught on the horns of a dilemma. She was pleased to see Barney so happy and grateful for the prospective income from Christmas geese sold for a handsome profit, but at the same time she was planning revenge. She thought about shutting the geese up in one of the numerous barns around the yard, but didn't relish the thought of cleaning up the copious amounts of manure produced by a little flock of geese. There were other good reasons for leaving them free; the food was virtually free, the grass mowing nil and prospective purchasers could see that their Christmas dinner was really free range when they came to call. They were also excellent guard dogs. The loss of chickens to foxes had been virtually nil since the geese had arrived. Even so, living with the beast had become impossible.

The morning ritual was perhaps as bad as it got, trying to get the children to the car, clutching slipper bags and lunch boxes, all trying to get behind Keeper's wife for protection whilst she brandished the yard brush at George, yelling abuse and dodging his hissing beak. She cursed as the children whimpered and planned all sorts of hideous revenge. Getting Keeper to shoot the blooming thing would be too good for him.

George was to solve the problem for her. One morning, when the morning mission to get the children to the school bus was almost accomplished without George noticing and having got the children safely into the car, George went too far. Keeper's wife backed the car out of the garage just as he spotted the invasion of his territory. He did his usual flying run at the car, wings flapping, honking so loud it hurt the ears.

In full flight, he attacked the reflection of a presumed invading gander pecking wildly at the hub cap of the departing car. From within the car the noise was terrifying, and the children held their breath waiting for Keeper's wife to explode in a fit of rage and verbal abuse. They cuddled into each other as Keeper's wife slammed the car into first and took off at tremendous speed down the gravel track, pebbles and dirt flying out the back of the car. Suddenly there was a slight bump as the car drove over something in the road, and then silence.

That had been George's final assault. In attacking his reflection his head had gone under the wheel of the car. Stopping the car, Keeper's wife got out to find a large gander with a very flat head in the road. She picked him up, in no doubt at all that he was dead, and hung him in the game store. Poor Barney was now a widow, and was likely to remain ever thus. One experience of a real fertile gander was enough for anyone.

Territorial behaviour

Why did George do it?

Territorial behaviour is built into the genes of ganders. That's why they make such a good substitute for guard dogs. They don't need to think there is an intruder or about being obnoxious – it just happens naturally in what's called a 'fixed action pattern' of behaviour. Any moving object that is even remotely unfamiliar in the yard, or anyone foolish enough to move too quickly, can act as a cue to the attack behaviour of a gander.

Once the behaviour is cued it must continue to the end, which is one of the rules of a fixed action pattern. For example, if a goose sees an egg outside her nest, she will reach forward and roll the egg towards the nest with her beak. At first glance this looks like intelligent behaviour. But believe me geese do not own one iota of intelligence. She is simply responding to the genetically wired-in behaviour she inherited. If you reach down and remove the egg, placing it again within reach of the goose, she will not stop what she is doing and reach out for the egg again. She will firstly have to continue rolling the now non-existent egg back into the nest before she can respond to the visual cue, the egg, again. They get stuck in a sort of behavioural loop that they cannot get out of. A bit like Saturday night after a football match when everyone knows how the row will turn out but no-one has the power to stop it.

Yum-Yum Corner
Cooking a goose and goose eggs

The eggs of geese are very rich and I think a little too strong for making a sponge. You can substitute them for hens' eggs in things like batter for pancakes or Yorkshire puddings or in custards. If you crack a goose egg and beat it, you will have the equivalent of three chicken eggs, so with any two-egg recipe you risk over-egging the pudding.

They are so delicious boiled or poached that it seems a shame to use them where you cannot tell it was a goose egg. You can use our methods for boiling, poaching, frying or scrambling, but you need to adjust for size. For example a boiled goose egg can take 10 minutes simmering in the pan, because not only are they bigger but the shell is much thicker. You need to experiment again with timing whilst you have lots of eggs.

Roast goose

You will need a deep roasting tin with a trivet so that the grease can drain out of the bird and not flood your oven. Preheat the oven to 180 and clean the bird inside and out. Put the giblets to one side for the gravy. Prick the bird all over so that the fat can escape. Geese have particular fat glands around the parson's nose and under the wings. Place the bird on the trivet and roast for around 3 hours for an 8-pound bird. Turn the bird over half way through the cooking time and drain off the fat into a bowl. This fat is fantastic for roast potatoes and other lovely things. It has also been used to waterproof Keeper's boots.

Testing to see if it is done is easy. You stick a skewer or very sharp knife into the fattest bit of the bird, such as the top of his leg. Press the hole you have made and the juices will run

Chapter Ten

out. If they are clear and not bloody, then your bird is ready for a 20-minute rest before you carve. If they are bloody, pop him back in for a bit.

You can experiment with all sorts of things like stuffing with chestnuts or parsley and thyme, wrapping in tin foil or flavouring with herbs and spices. I never stuff a bird before roasting. I think it slows down the cooking time and risks the meat being dry. I never add anything to the meat either. I can't see the point of waiting a year to eat your goose and then drowning out the flavour with lemon grass and 5-spice. You are allowed to season though, especially the roast potatoes.

Research
Finding out about fat with the children

Can you buy goose fat? See how much goose fat is……
Can you buy duck fat? See how much duck fat is…….

Fat is what we use to make roast potatoes. There are lots of different kinds of fat. An old favourite is lard. This is usually made from pig fat. It is very pure and clean. It can be used for frying, roasting, pastry and other things we bake.

When we cook meat, the fat renders (melts) out. We call this dripping. Dripping is not pure and often has a delicious jelly set at the bottom. This can be used for frying or roasting. My grandad used to spread this on toast and sprinkle it liberally with salt. Oil is another thing we use to fry and roast things like fish and chips.

Next time you go to the supermarket take that notebook with you and see if you can find examples of oil, lard and dripping. Write down what they cost. It's hard to work out which is most economical because they all come in different amounts, but you could take a guess.

You get both of these expensive products free when you cook a duck or goose by rendering the fat as they cook. It will be cheaper to practise with pork.

Experiment: making lard and crackling

See if you can buy a piece of pork fat with the skin on it. You can make two very delicious things from this. Use a modelling knife to cut grooves in the skin about a centimetre apart.

Sprinkle with salt and rub it into the grooves. Then put it into the oven in a roasting dish at about 140° for several hours. When the fat has disappeared into the liquid and the skin is crisp and brown, it is done. Strain the liquid to remove any pieces and put to set in a cold place. You have now made lard. It might not be pure enough to bake with, but it will be yummy for frying and roasting.

Take a sharp knife and cut the crispy remains of the skin into strips. Season with sea salt and you have made crackling. This is better than crisps and not the same as scratchings that you buy in the pub, which are not made from the skin of the pig.

Goosey goosey gander,
Where shall I wander?
Upstairs and downstairs
And in my lady's chamber.
There I met an old man
Who wouldn't say his prayers,
So I took him by his left leg
And threw him down the stairs.
The stairs went crack, he broke his little back
And all the little duckies went quack, quack, quack.

Chapter Eleven

Guinea fowl as guard dogs

Guinea fowl as guard dogs

When George died Barney went downhill fast, and we lost her one November day. There was now no one to sound the alarm when two or four-legged prowlers were about. Keeper's wife asked for guinea fowl for Christmas. They are very noisy and make fantastic guard dogs.

A trio duly arrived and worked extremely well. They were very noisy when visitors arrived, shouting 'come back, come back, come back,' and roosted high up in the old yew tree out of harm's way at night. From this vantage point they could survey the entire yard and create their own unmistakable racket whenever we returned home or they were alarmed.

Learning about guinea fowl

Guinea fowl originated in West Africa and were once called 'pet speckled hens'. They are quite like partridges but much bigger. They are a sort of cross between a peacock and a pheasant to look at. They are ground nesting birds and eat insects and seeds. They are also monogamous. That means they mate for life and are very faithful. Their eating habits are YUK. They are brilliant foragers, a bit like vultures, poking their beaks into anything you would find revolting like horse manure, cow dung and dog poo. They love to find dead rotting bodies and poke about in carcasses looking for maggots. They don't drink very much. Perhaps this is why their meat is dry. This is why I don't like eating them, but at least they are free range and happy.

They were once wild, but are now

reared for their meat. You can buy it in supermarkets and they weigh between 1-3 pounds. They are reared both free range and intensively, so you need to check before you buy because I know you wouldn't buy anything that was intensively reared. They also lay decent eggs. These are peculiar, as they have a very pointed end. They are also very, very hard. Not easy to crack or peel if you hard boil them. Good to tease visitors with if you serve them in the shell. No tap, tap, tap with a spoon to get inside. You're more likely to get in if you crack it with a hammer.

They are brilliant yard birds, and almost take care of themselves. They are very strong fliers and often roost right at the top of trees. The only danger time for them is when they are brooding eggs or keeping young warm. They are always on the alert for danger and make the most horrific noise if anything comes into their yard. One of them screaming the guinea alert is ear piercing. Can you imagine the din when eight or nine of them go off together? You need ear plugs to stay in the yard very long. The good points are that their steering is better than Muscovies and they don't poo as much.

Back to the yard

The following year both females disappeared into the under growth for a long time and emerged within days of each other with broods of chicks. They then became banshees, screaming about the yard whenever anyone or anything went near the chicks.

They barely stood still long enough for us to count how many guinea fowl we now had. It was about this time that the birds began appearing in the supermarket, a fact that signalled to Keeper's wife that they must be good eating.

Once full grown they became a real nuisance. Their droppings were tainting the ground under the yew tree and woe betide anyone foolish enough to park their car under the tree. They were also a terrifying sight as the whole flock of them flew at you whenever you tried to go out in the car or hang out a bit of washing. They would have to go.

Roald Dahl's pheasant poaching trick

The discovery that they were fetching a good price at market sealed their fate. However, getting them out of the yew tree and catching them was going to be the very devil. Being a Roald Dahl fan, the pheasant poaching story in Danny, the Champion of the World came to mind. In this story pheasants are fed raisins with sleeping tablets hidden inside. These were quickly gobbled up by the birds. Finding a pound or so of raisins in the pantry, Keeper's wife put the fruit in a basin. Not having sleeping pills to hand, she soaked the raisins with enough vodka to cover, leaving them to become alcoholic overnight.

Late the following evening the guinea fowl were given their luxurious alcoholic supper. They loved it, ate their fill and flew up the tree to roost for the night. Keeper's wife gave them 20 minutes and then came out with the crates, a long pole and a net. One by one the birds began their drunken descent from the yew, encouraged by a poke up the backside with a long pole. They were hysterically funny, fluttering clumsily to the ground and looking totally bemused but very happy.

Working quickly to beat the dark, the family set about catching the young fowl and crating them up in trios ready for market tomorrow. They were easier to catch than to sex. A trio should consist of one male and two females. The only thing Keeper's Wife would be happy to guarantee was that each trio consisted of three birds. Ah. Back to the original trio of birds.

Chapter Eleven

Yum-Yum Corner
Roast guinea fowl and stuffing

Cooking guinea fowl is pretty much like cooking chicken. It does have a tendency to be a bit dry, so it really suffers from over cooking. It needs lots of basting and stays really moist if you put butter under the breast skin and streaky bacon over the breast before it goes in the oven. It goes brilliantly with everything in our hedgerows in the autumn, like blackberries, cobnuts, pine kernels, apples, plums or chestnuts. You can use these in sauces or stuffings. One guinea is perfect for two people.

It needs to be at room temperature before it goes in the oven. This cuts down cooking time and reduces the risk of being dry. Use the same rules as for chicken, 15 minutes for the bird and 15 for each pound. Use the smallest possible tray so that the bird is not exposed to too much all round heat. Test it is done by sticking a skewer into the fattest bit to see if the juices run clear, just as we did with the chicken.

I never put the stuffing in the cavity, but herbs are OK, they don't slow down the cooking, just add lots of flavour. You can put the stuffing in the tray with the bird so it absorbs some of the juices. This can protect the wings and legs as well. Save the remaining juices for the gravy.

If the bird is old you can casserole or boil in our usual way. If you have any red wine you could do coq au vin.

Research
Finding out about bones and gravy

Next time you go to the supermarket with the children, take your notebook with you. Take a good look at the stocks and stock cubes.

How many different kinds of stock cubes do they have?
How many different kinds do they have?
Can you buy bones to make your own stock?

If they don't sell bones you might have to find a proper butcher. My butcher sells all types of bones. In the summer when he is making things for customers to barbecue he sells the chicken carcasses after he has taken off the legs, wings and breasts. These are fantastic for stock.

The bone experiment

If you can get chicken and lamb bones you could experiment with these to see which you prefer.

To get the best out of your bones you need to cook them twice. You begin by chopping them into small pieces and then browning them. This can be done in the oven in a roasting tin for an hour or so or in a deep frying pan. When they are nicely brown put them in a big saucepan with carrots, onions and celery. Pour boiling water over the juices and remains in the pan you cooked the bones in, and scrape all the dark bits off the bottom. This is where all the flavour is. Pour this over your bones. Now is the time to add herbs, seasonings and anything else you have hanging around to add taste. Bacon rind is good.

Chapter Eleven

Half a bottle of wine is also good. Red for lamb, white for chicken, so they say.

Simmer gently for half an hour and taste. The longer you simmer the richer the stock will get. Be careful of the salt content. If you are going to cook it for a long time the liquid will reduce and anything you added at the beginning of the cook will intensify. Keep tasting.

Which do you prefer, chicken or lamb stock?

Make a cup of stock using a shop bought cube. Which do you prefer now?

What will you do with your stock now?

The Guinea Fowl

There is a sort of feathered scold
Whose note is (if the truth be told)
Much like a vixen's clack,
Morn, noon, and night the sound you hear,
Still ringing in your deafened ear,
"Come back! Come back! Come back!"
When forced to leave a pleasant home,
Upon the world's wide waste to roam,
Our sinking hearts alack!
Feel all their devils doubly blue,
If some of this discordant crew
Cry out, "Come back! Come back!"
But if with travel, toil and pain
Worn out, we're hastening home again,
Our fancy has a knack …

Guinea fowl as guard dogs

Of making even discord sweet,
Which seems our own return to greet,
With Wel—"come back, come back!"
My song, much like the throat it mocks,
As shrill as winds and hard as rocks,
(Since rhyme is growing slack)
As it began perforce must end
By crying out with every friend
"Come back! come back! come back!"
- Richard Henry Wilde

The Guinea Fowl

The guinea fowl counts: one, two, three, four ...
Pray what is all that counting for,
Out there among the deep dark pine trees?
The bird, driven by knowledge's itch,
And doing so without a glitch,
Is counting what it's worth in guineas.
- Christian Morgenstern (1871-1914)

A guinea in old money was one pound and one shilling. It was currency often used to purchase stock and is still used today at horse sales.

Chapter Eleven

Well grandchildren!

There are many more of you than there were many years ago when these stories began. We have passed through the Chinese year of the rooster five times since the beginning of these stories. We have discovered lots about chickens and other types of poultry that we didn't know, and I hope you have come to understand the importance of the welfare of the chicken and eggs that you are going to eat.

Remember if you feed chickens rubbish food you will get rubbish eggs, and rubbish eggs are not as good for you as beautiful free-range shiny healthy eggs from healthy chickens.

From chucky to guinea fowl we have learned many secrets of poultry. We have learned how to care for the eggs, hatch the eggs, care for the chicks. And we have learned that we can love and care for chickens that will one day be dinner.

I hope you take this book to university with you and share this knowledge with your friends and convert them into chicken and egg lovers. And for those of you starting a family, look for ways of advancing your egg cooking skills and feed your children well. And remember eggs can go into everything, even Christmas cake!

When feeding the ducks at the duck pond, please buy corn at your local pet shop. The diet for ducks is not white bread! Feed them well so that they can make healthy eggs and healthy ducklings.

One day we hope no chickens will live in tiny cages and not be able to recognise their own eggs and that all the chickens we buy to eat will have tasted grubs and worms and grass, and perhaps had a chance to roost in a tree, or even become guard dogs like the gander and the guinea fowl, keeping everyone in the yard safe.

Goodnight everyone.
Ann D

www.ingramcontent.com/pod-product-compliance
Lightning Source LLC
Chambersburg PA
CBHW041153230426
43673CB00036B/505